DATE DUE

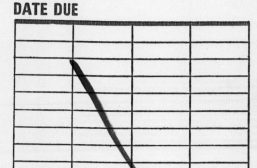

The English Church
A New Look

Edited by
LESLIE S. HUNTER

with contributions by
EDWARD F. CARPENTER
ALFRED JOWETT
T. R. MILFORD
MAX WARREN
EDWARD R. WICKHAM
LESLIE S. HUNTER

PENGUIN BOOKS
BALTIMORE · MARYLAND

Penguin Books Ltd, Harmondsworth, Middlesex, England
Penguin Books Inc., 3300 Clipper Mill Road, Baltimore 11, Md, U.S.A.
Penguin Books Pty Ltd, Ringwood, Victoria, Australia

—

First published 1966

—

Copyright © Penguin Books Ltd, 1966

—

Made and printed in Great Britain
by Hazell Watson & Viney Ltd, Aylesbury, Bucks
Set in Monotype Garamond

CONTENTS

THE PRAYER FOR PARLIAMENT

ALMIGHTY God, by whom alone Kings reign, and Princes decree justice; and from whom alone cometh all counsel, wisdom, and understanding; We thine unworthy servants, here gathered together in thy Name, do most humbly beseech thee to send down thy Heavenly Wisdom from above, to direct and guide us in all our consultations: And grant that, we having thy fear always before our eyes, and laying aside all private interests, prejudices, and partial affections, the result of all our counsels may be to the glory of thy blessed Name, the maintenance of true Religion and Justice, the safety, honour, and happiness of the Queen, the publick wealth, peace and tranquillity of the Realm, and the uniting and knitting together of the hearts of all persons and estates within the same, in true Christian Love and Charity one towards another, through Jesus Christ our Lord and Saviour.

Amen

Each day's sitting of the House of Commons and of the House of Lords begins with prayers read in the Chamber: in the Commons by the Speaker's Chaplain, in the Lords by one of the Bishops with a seat in the House. The doors are shut and no strangers are admitted until, with the cry 'Prayers are over', the door-keepers open the doors. The form has been invariable since 1661. Psalm 67 is read and then follow prayers from the Book of Common Prayer with a Prayer for Parliament, which was written by an unknown author in 1661.

INTRODUCTION AND PREFACE

THIS book is about the relationship of the Christian Church and the English People, and more particularly about the Establishment. The subject is important because this inheritance goes back for over a thousand years of English history and beyond that to the Apostolic Church and to the Bible, which is for Christians the textbook for religious truth and good living. But it is chiefly as an important contemporary issue that the subject will be discussed in this book. Great and rapid changes are happening in thought and life which will determine the future of the nation and also the influence of the Church of England in it and in the life of the world.

At varying tempo in different countries society is moving from an agricultural civilization, which has characterized European life for over 2,000 years, into an industrialized and urbanized era. This is going to be a more radical change than that from the nomadic to the agricultural pattern of life, which is, for example, reflected in the early chapters of the Bible. It is a process commensurate with life itself, influencing persons and communities whether they are conscious of it or not. In these last decades it is reaching a climax, changing the climate of thought and the cultural pattern of day-to-day living. 'The task of Christians', the Dean of Manchester (who contributes a chapter in this book) wrote the other day, 'is to take the lead in helping the whole community to identify their problems and to move towards a genuinely human solution of them.' Whether they can will depend in this country not a little on the relationship of Church and State and the form it may take in the years immediately ahead. The following chapters argue the first and attempt to outline the second.

A scientific revolution and a social revolution have been converging. The former dates from three centuries ago when men began to study, weigh, and compare observable facts ex-

9

actly, and to make generalizations and hypotheses to account for them – with free and open minds. This new scientific discipline has led to a continuous expansion of man's knowledge both of the universe and of himself, and consequently to a stupendous increase of power to use and control the matter of the universe. It is not an exaggerated claim that a scientist was making when he wrote: 'Society is being moulded in a new pattern by scientific discovery and its application in technology and social engineering.'[1]

The social revolution in this country was not motivated at first by science, but by the Hebrew prophets and the Christian ethic. As late as the end of last century some of its exponents like William Morris were so horrified by the ugliness and cruelty of industry that they cried passionately for a return to a more primitive and rural way of life. But science, technology and social engineering have now taken over the guiding reins. Society, in spite of two world wars, has made immense progress since the age when 'Adam delved and Eve span' and both had to work unceasingly to keep famine and disease, nature and human enemies from the door.

And yet that is not the whole story. Even on the level of material progress and social engineering there have been setbacks. Time and again a civilized society, just when crowns and a queendom were in sight, has been put back to square one by forces hostile to its advance towards wholeness of life, both within itself, and may be also from without. It may happen again now that Man has gained the power to destroy both himself and his world.

H. A. L. Fisher begins the epilogue to his great *History of Europe* with this reflection, 'After some twenty million years of life on this planet the lot of the major part of humanity is still, as Hobbes once described it, "nasty, brutish and short" '.[2] The 'twenty millions' is a bit rhetorical, for most of it belongs to pre-history about which we know very little. Nevertheless, human nature does not seem to have improved on itself very much. Egoism, pride, sloth, as well as the more obvious vices will take a lot of eradicating. The Kingdom of Truth and Love, which we trust is the consummation of the cosmic process and of man's journey, is a long way off from where human society is. Scientific man in an industrial age perhaps needs even more than nomadic man and agricultural man a faith to live by which will sustain his purpose and courage. To bring the thought down to earth and the contemporary scene, let me quote some words which fell from an economist a few months ago,

It is inevitable that there must be a greater emphasis on government and management by consent, with adult behaviour by consent, and with a management aware of its social responsibilities. An automatic plant cannot be run in any other way.

He was speaking of this country whose society seems to have become so intoxicated by the new affluence that all groups are demanding more and more for doing less and less – with continuous inflation, both cause and consequence. No amount of automation and cybernation in factories and labour-saving gadgets in homes will make an economy viable so long as this mentality persists. It may look as though mammon had made a successful take-over bid and that the long-standing antagonism has been liquidated; but the writing on the wall is still faintly there for him who pauses to read. The 'either-or' of the Lord of life is ineluctable. A wholesome society cannot *worship* God and mammon; and a man does not need to be a puritan to recognize it.

What the puritans did not understand and modern man must is that he has to learn to live and work *in community* in order to use the resources now at his disposal, or else he will be destroyed by them. He will have to choose between accepting this social discipline of his own free will or submitting to its exercise by an over-riding authority. In that choice a religion with a social ethic may prove to have a decisive part to play.

One feature of the urbanized, industrial society that has been created by science and technology is the weakening hold of all the classic religions and the declining influence of the ecclesiastical institutions which have been their expression. This is true of the Christian Church and of religious observances in Europe. In parenthesis one would say that it is also true that in the early days of scientific thought Christianity was its matrix. Our hope is that in spite of the controversies of the nineteenth century and the questions which science poses for theology in the more free and open discussions since, Christian faith may eventually walk in – armed with science in the new society. It will not do, however, to be too lightly optimistic, for agnosticism, which used to be discreetly covered, has risen to the surface and exploded in society with some violence; while a new phenomenon in history is the militant godless man exemplified by Marx, Nietzsche and Sartre.

What then is the future of religious institutions? Will they maintain their traditional patterns only to serve a minority? Can an established church be so invigorated with new life as to give the new society a faith to live by? Before these questions can be fairly answered the causes of the decline must be examined. This theological and sociological enquiry extends far beyond the limits of this book. Here only two factors in addition to the one just referred to may be mentioned. In the past one powerful motive of conventional religious observance and also of much superstition was the desire to win the favour of the gods and get providence on the worshipper's side. Now that in many aspects of life man has become his own providence this motive has greatly weakened. It was not always easy to disentangle this conventional self-centred religion from a true faith that makes a man forget himself and say 'great is truth', and more personally, 'not my will but thine be done'. In the new society one would expect the distinction to become clearer, and also that between 'conventional wisdom' and Christian insights and judgements. If so, the decline would be quantitative; and the effective influence of the Church strengthened.

Again, in countries like Britain the state has been taking

over social services which once were rendered by the Church when it gave to medical service on battlefields the emblem and inspiration of the Cross, and often stood to orphans *in loco parentis* and was a channel of charity towards those who fell by the way. The modern state, influenced originally by the Christian ethic, enters more and more intimately into its citizens' personal and family life, and is able to do more thoroughly with its financial resources and the skills it can command what Church and voluntary agencies could only do partially. This change involves a new type of partnership between church and state at all levels which must be worked out.

It is not within the compass of this book to discuss fully these and similar questions and issues, but it is written with a lively awareness of their importance, and also with the conviction that such actualities as the national Church and its continuing establishment are relevant to the debate and to a right solution. At first glance some may think this is not so and that the heritage is part of the left luggage of the agricultural era, like some of our cultural inheritance. It inevitably bears the impress of that long span in the life of man. Nevertheless, although some thought-forms like the furniture and buildings which served in feudal times may be outmoded and have had their day, the Christian faith by which and on which the Church has stood remains valid. The activity of God in life is not a 'has-been' and religious institutions and liturgies are one channel of that activity. The argument which this book pursues is that the basic pattern of the church–state relationship is as necessary to the health and vitality of both as ever it was. If confidence is one motive for its argument so is a fear that some who pride themselves on being down-to-date may regard national churches and establishment as obsolete. In a time of change it is indeed dangerous to be too nostalgic about the past or too apprehensive of the future. The Spirit of God is still operative; and the new knowledge and the enrichment of life that science and technology have brought have his hall-mark. The members of the Church have to discover what he is at and prepare themselves to be a sword in his hand.

This book also has to argue with a piety that in a 'secular age' regards the church–state relationship and establishment as dangerously erastian and worldly. They can be and often have been – *corruptio optimi pessima*. '*Optimi*' – yes! This book argues at some depth the case for our inheritance in the Church of England, its value today, and also for tomorrow if it is able to be flexible and moving. The argument is not novel. Some far-sighted churchmen, to go no further back than last century, have voiced it. Thus Frederick Denison Maurice, a prophet of the middle of that century, wrote,

A national Church should mean a Church which exists to purify and elevate the mind of a nation, to give those who make and administer and obey its laws a sense of the grandness of law and of the source whence it proceeds, to tell the rulers of the nation and the members of the nation that all false ways are ruinous ways, that truth is the only stability of our time or of any time.[3]

And again,

There are many Christians who would persuade us that the life of a nation is what they call a secular thing – – – – I solemnly deny that a Nation is a secular thing – – – – One of the greatest weapons God has given us is the assurance that the Nation has lived, lives now, and will live in him who was and is, and is to come.[4]

Alongside this we would set what the great Free Church theologian, an Aberdonian by birth, Principal P. T. Forsyth, wrote in 1915,

Both (Church and State) are divine agents for human perfection. But the one by way of conscience and its redemption. The State does not exist to make men good, the Church does. The State to secure the conditions of goodness, the Church to create the thing itself . . . the State is an agent of the Kingdom of God, the Church is the Kingdom of God in the making. . . . To take the name of a Church is really to assume such a relationship to the nation as cannot be indifferent to the State, nor observe a mere neutrality.[5]

Forty years later – and what momentous years they were! – Archbishop Fisher in the course of his enthronement sermon in Canterbury said,

The responsibility of the Catholic Church is always and altogether to our Lord Jesus Christ in whom the Church consists. It is within and as part of that catholic responsibility that the Church of England is also the national church of this country. . . . Its distinguishing characteristic is that in loyalty to Christ it endeavours to hold together in a due proportion, truths which, though essential to the fullness of the Gospel of Christ, are through the frailness of man's spirit not easily combined . . . But it is the conviction and justification of this Church of England that Christ means us to essay this difficult comprehension . . . and to present as far as we may, the wholeness of the Gospel of Christ.

Church and nation have grown up together, and we see God's providence at work in both. The stresses within the Church, and the unifying loyalty that controls them, have their counterpart in our secular history . . . And the unifying forces have their roots and strength in that heritage of Christian faith which the Church has implanted and preserved among us through the centuries.[6]

A book written by one person is generally more readable than a symposium. It seemed good, however, to the editor of this one to invite the cooperation of men, distinguished in the Christian ministry, who have more expertise in regard to some aspects of the subject than he has, and more scholarship.

We have had discussion with one another and with others about the contents of the book. We share a love of this Church of England, and are in agreement as to the direction it should be looking and moving. Each writer, however, is only responsible for what he has written and not for what the others have written. In so far as any one has an over-all responsibility it must be the editor who projected the book and has seen it through the press with the much appreciated help and advice of Mr Dieter Pevsner of Penguin Books Ltd.

The chapters reflect differences both in diagnosis and prescription. This is as it should be in a Church that is catholic and comprehensive and knows that it is entrusted with a Gospel for the whole world. We have had to limit ourselves to one aspect of the Church's life and work in one country – and say nothing about the Church of England's share in the expansion of Christianity in other lands, or, for example, about its dialogue with Buddhism or Communism.

The several chapters have a natural sequence and are held together by a common theme:

After a short discussion of basic issues, come two historical studies. The Master of the Temple, Canon Dick Milford, who has had years of experience of debate on the Christian frontiers in India and in this country, writes significantly about the Bible; and then Edward Carpenter, Archdeacon of Westminster Abbey, a lively Christian apologist these days in London, writes about the Church–State relationship in English history. Next, the Editor, who was Bishop of Sheffield for nearly twenty-three years and has lived and worked most of his life in the industrial areas of the country, writes on Episcopacy, and later in the book on the Economy of the Church of England, a subject which he has studied and on which he has spoken and written a good deal.

The chapter on Episcopacy is followed by one on the Church in the local situation by Alfred Jowett, who was for many years a vicar in Sheffield and Doncaster, and is now Dean of Manchester. To this is appended a long note by the editor, for which he is considerably in debt to the Bishop of Taunton (the Rt Rev. F. H. West), on the Church and country life.

Next, Canon Max Warren – and there is no English Churchman more travelled than the former Secretary of the Church Missionary Society, or any who has travelled with a more perceptive eye – contributes what seems at first to be a refreshing breeze from over the seas, but nonetheless a study that is obliquely but truly related to our theme. Finally, or very nearly finally, the Bishop of Middleton, better known as Ted Wickham, who fashioned the Sheffield Industrial Mission, and understands at depth industrial society, provides what my fellow-Scots would call 'a deliverance' on the New Look. To all these very busy friends, the editor gives his warm thanks.

The theme and the conclusion are quite simply that a paramount need of countries with a long Christian tradition is a re-formulation of Christian belief and a re-invigorated practice which will give men a world-view and enable them to be integrated personalities living peaceably in communities. This aim requires of the national Church a re-formation at depth of its life and a new sense of mission. In order to bring home to a divided world and to every man the relevance of the Gospel of Jesus Christ, the divided parts of the Church in this and all lands must grow together so that their unity is visible for all men to see. In this direction, also, a national church, to be true to its name, must be looking and leading the way.

L. S. H.

NOTES

1. Professor F. E. Simon, *The Neglect of Science*. Cf. also H. Butterfield, Professor of Modern History in the University of Cambridge, *Origins of Modern Science*, p. viii, 'the so-called "scientific revolution" . . . outshines everything since the rise of Christianity and reduces the Renaissance and Reformation to the rank of mere episodes, mere internal displacements, within the system of medieval Christendom, since it changed the character of men's habitual mental operations, even in the conduct of the non-material sciences, while transforming the whole diagram of the physical universe and of the very texture of human life itself, it looms so large as the real origin of the modern world and the modern mentality.'

2. H. A. L. Fisher, *A History of Europe*, Vol. III, p. 1219.

3. F. D. Maurice. *Lincoln Inn Sermons*, Vol. II. These quotations may be found in Vidler, *Maurice's Message for Today*, S.C.M. Press, which was first published by Scribner's in U.S.A. under the title *Witness to the Light*.

4. Maurice, *Hope for Mankind*, p. 45 and cf. *Prophets and Kings*, p. 403.

5. P. T. Forsyth, *Theology in Church and State*, pp. 255 & 237, quoted in A. C. Vidler's *The Orb and the Cross*. The whole of Vidler's book, which is a study and reflection on Gladstone's writing is relevant to our subject.

6. Geoffrey Fisher, Enthronement Sermon in Canterbury Cathedral, 19 April 1945. Reprinted in C. H. Smyth, *The Church and the Nation*, Hodder & Stoughton, 1962.

SOME BASIC ISSUES

1 *Church and Society*

THE relationship between the Church and English society is not what it was. The Church's sphere of influence has become more restricted; that of the State has widened. Although the majority of the population has been baptized, married and buried by ministers of the Church of England, it is not easy to assess, and opinions will differ, how much such conformity signifies. Both the Christian faith, and what is thought to be Christian ethics are being disregarded, and not only by the thoughtless. Let churchmen be realist about this. At the same time they should not jump to the conclusion that a numerically declining Church is becoming more like the Kingdom of God, and the nation and a state, which is beginning to look to scientists and technologists for guidance rather than to bishops and denominational secretaries, are moving in the opposite direction.

There are several considerations that qualify such a judgement. When statisticians seem to evaluate a human situation by counting heads without reference to what is going on inside them, it is well to remember that history is a very selective account of the life of human society. The vast majority of those who have lived and died have left no memorial behind them. For knowledge of their way of life the historian is dependent on the rare few who have, while the palaeontologists have to deduce what they can about pre-historic man from fossils. Often it is difficult even for the trained and imaginative historian to see through the scanty records written by educated men to the kind of life that the uneducated majority was living and to what its thoughts and operative beliefs were.

Churchmen should also remember some facts about their

own history. The writers of the Old Testament in the course of several centuries belonged to a small minority of the Hebrew people who quite accurately described themselves at one period as a 'remnant'. The committed followers of Jesus in Palestine during his short ministry were only a little group in a small population. The number of disciples who met in an upper room before Pentecost is given as a hundred-and-twenty. The number increased quickly after Pentecost; but two or three centuries later the churches scattered over the larger cities of the Roman Empire were also only a fractional part of their populations. Nevertheless – and this is the point to note – it was these small groups of faithful men and women, fired by the Spirit of God, who left a memorial behind them, moulded the thoughts and lives of succeeding generations and dictated the course of history in Europe. The operative words in that sentence are not 'small groups', but 'fired by the Spirit of God'.

Nevertheless, it is an indubitable fact of history that we owe our spiritual and cultural inheritance to a very small minority even in Christendom. That minority, however, did not consist of huddle-minded pessimists, but of men and women alive unto God, on their toes, so to say, ready to run anywhere in the world on his errands, or, alternatively, not to run at all except in prayer.

Those who see the Church as an instrument of God's purpose, and are trying to love his world and the people in it must not let their hope and courage be shaken by those who like to contrast the number of Easter communicants with the number who do football pools on a Sunday or point out in tones menacing to the parochial clergy that there has been 'a drop in the number of Christian burials last year'. All that kind of pseudo-sociology, especially when it is inspired by gnosticism rather than by Christian faith, might in these days of advertising psychology and salesmanship set reformers off on the wrong foot even if it does not set them off in the wrong direction.

Churchmen – as well as others – have to analyse, and assess

secularization – before, despairingly, they retreat to the cata-combs or self-righteously vote for cutting the communications between church and state. Their assessment might be more sensitive to true values – more truly 'in Christ' as St Paul would say – if their analysis were not in terms of the institutional church over against a secular society, but in terms of the Kingdom of God and life, enriched as it now is by the massive contribution of science and technology.

Moreover, the distinction between Church and the world, which was clear to the fourth evangelist when Christianity was beginning to penetrate pagan society and Christians were being persecuted for their enterprise, is not so clear in a society where Christianity has been an integrating and edu-cative power for over a thousand years. Today 'the children of the world' and 'the children of light' are not a little con-fused – partly because the same man and group may belong to both categories. The children of the world may not only be wiser than the children of light as Jesus said; they may often show a Christian sensitivity and decision that puts the others to shame. All too often, though not as often as some allege, the non-church-goer may prove a better neighbour and a more responsible workman than some who do go. Piety, and its domestic arrangements have often, since the Reformation and Counter-Reformation, put blinkers on churchy men and women. Religion has had its moral dangers as well as its triumphs. (Admitting all that, the writer must, in order to be true to his own experience, interpolate that it is wonderful and heartening to meet in many parts of the world, far from one another, and in spite of differences of language, nationality and environment, and in spite of the broken unity of the Church, the family likeness of those who share the Christian faith. That realization of unity in Christ is so arresting that quickly and not impermanently a friendship grows, which prayer keeps warm, although the chances of meeting again in this life lessen as the years slip by.)

Many of the issues of our time, moreover, that are most momentous for the welfare of mankind are those which confront men in the course of their 'secular' work; and on which decisions are taken at meetings that do not open with vocal prayer. Daily, in industry, trade, banking, government and the professions, men are carrying responsibility for other men and their families and are acting on behalf of them most honourably. Compared with these issues many matters discussed at church committees and councils are of little importance. This area of 'secular obedience' is for Christian men the field for the exercise of Christian insights and loyalties, and often in this secular field men who might hesitate to call themselves churchmen are acting more Christianly than they know.

Those who try to make a sharp distinction between secular and sacred overlook the fact that the Old Testament is by that standard a very secular book and reveals a rather secular deity. The Hebrew prophets were laymen whose understanding of God made them care very much about human relationships and social justice. They found in the nation's 'home affairs' and 'foreign policy' fields where God's will operated. The books of the Law in the O.T. cover such matters as in a modern state are dealt with by Ministers of Health, Education, Labour, Home Office and Board of Trade, as well as the life of the family. The Wisdom Literature ranges over every aspect of a people's life. The people of God looked for a Messiah, not of the house of Aaron, but a descendant of King David; similarly, the New Testament into which the Old Testament leads. The Incarnation consecrates the whole life of man and not only that part that is 'religious'. The Kingdom that the Lord Jesus realized and proclaimed is a quality and way of life permeating and transforming the whole life of society.

Therefore, as a society in the world and committed to 'the evangelization of the world', the Church cannot limit its action to preaching or to praying that 'the course of this world may be so peaceably ordered that the Church may serve thee in all godly quietness'. It has also to try to secure that the political and economic structure of society helps rather than hinders the good life. Christians are indebted to Karl Marx for making them more aware that the economic pattern and pressures in an industrial society are stronger and more controlling than religious idealists have supposed. In other words Christians have not only to sow the good seed, they have to cooperate with others to ensure that the soil is receptive and fertile.

What about 'establishment' in relation to this? To those who are forward looking, or like to think they are, the word suggests the backward glance, a static posture, even freedom in chains. Applied to the relations of Church and State in this country it means 'not that the Church is identified with the State, nor that the Church is a department of the State, but that the Church is formally accredited by the State to bear the *persona* of the nation in its religious aspect, and to lead the nation in prayers'; or in Canon Max Warren's words, 'strictly speaking establishment means recognition.'[7]

In this island the Church gave the pagan colonizers from Northern Europe a faith to live by in a new situation, and so it became the godfather of the growing Anglo-Saxon kingdom. It sanctified its law, hallowed its kingship and set a way of life for ruler and ruled. In a subsequent chapter Canon Carpenter outlines the continuing history of this partnership which is woven into the British constitution. This inheritance is unique, for the relationship is in many ways dissimilar from that in other European countries. In the Scandinavian countries, for example, the Lutheran Church is so tied to the State that there is a Minister for Church Affairs in the government, and his department deals with that proportion of the national income which is 'the church tax'. In other European countries there are similar tax arrangements; according to the ratio of church membership to population the tax may be allocated to Orthodox, Roman Catholic and Protestant Communions. In England, income from taxation does not pass to the established Church; if we were starting *de novo* no one would be likely to think up the intimate and flexible relationship that we have. Like other things of value in the working of the British Constitution it depends, as a recent report[8] has pointed out, on a lot of personal goodwill – not an unchristian thing to depend on provided the techniques of the relationship allow for partnership and free association.

In any society responsible positions that provide opportunities for service can be misused so that they become merely privileges. The Church being composed of sinners is no exception. Its representatives have often failed in this respect. It was so in medieval times when the clerisy provided the civil service and many of the executives of the Sovereign's government; and after the Reformation era abuse of responsibility and power provoked the bitterness of dissent. National Churches, especially, have been hurt in their witness to 'Christ, the Servant' when government in church and state have been associated with privilege, and the ruling class has been a small minority.

If the Church–State partnership is to continue beneficially in this country, the Church of England must cleanse vestiges of privilege from the opportunities of service – at all levels. That should not be so difficult to do in a democratic country when State and People are becoming more aware of the distinction between privilege and responsibility. Our inheritance is precious, not because it confers privileges, but because it entrusts the Church of England with unique opportunities of service, which are shared indeed with the State and local authorities, and might before long be shared in a Church in which conformist and non-conformist can worship together.

2 *Church and Churches*

Those who guided the thought and policy of the Church of England after the break with the Papacy in the sixteenth century hoped that it might comprehend all English Christians and be the nation at prayer. They had of course no illusions about the number of people in any generation who are in their practice godless and worldly. The hope of achieving Christian unity was quite defeated; and for centuries Christians in England have been divided into conformists and non-conformists. Today with the growth of ecumenicity on the one hand and of secularism on the other the hope of unity has revived and the prospects of reunion are being explored. A realistic discussion of the future of a national Church must share this hope and take account of the possibility of reunion.

The greater misfortune for the faith and spiritual life of England in the twentieth century has not been the continuance of non-conformity but its decline from the time of its strength a century and more ago. If one considers objectively the spiritual vitality of the English people in those days, and especially if one compares it with the spiritual torpor of some European countries where there was an established church and no vigorous non-conformity, one must allow that the divided state of the Church in those days was not contrary to the divine will. Methodism would not have been the power it was had it not snapped its fingers at the ecclesiastical raj. The influence of congregations such as Carr's Lane Birmingham, St James' Newcastle-on-Tyne, Trinity Church Glasgow, Spurgeon's Tabernacle and the City Temple in London, owed much to their independency. And what shall we say of the contribution to the Christian life of England by the families that gathered in Friends Meeting Houses, or the devout loyalty of those who for generations had been Roman Catholics? The flame of the Free Churches might not have burnt so strongly if they had not been able to strike light on the flinty walls of the Establishment – and the Establishment might not have woken out of its eighteenth-century torpor – had it not been alerted by Dissent. And it would be unrealistic to deny that many people have found, and as far as we can foresee will continue to find, a satisfying spiritual nourishment in free forms of worship and a non-sacramental liturgical order like Morning and Evening Prayer.

One danger to be guarded against is that the real laity should be stampeded by a clerisy which is thinking too narrowly in terms of ecclesiastical order and would too willingly sacrifice truth on the altar of ecumenicity. This is a more real danger than some enthusiasts for unity allow, for it would be *pari passu* with what is happening in the world. While in British democracy an essential part has been Her Majesty's Opposition, elsewhere the pressures are towards single-party government and dictatorships. The movement towards reunion, therefore, must be wise and not too contemptuous or ignorant of history: some of the wisdom will have to be the courage to be illogical and to allow not only for diversity but even for contradiction. The Church of England knows a good deal about this: and in its life comprehensiveness has been a strength rather than a weakness.

It is possible to allow for all this and at the same time to agree with William Temple when he said at his enthronement in Canterbury Cathedral in 1942: 'In preparation for a time such as this God has been building up a Christian fellowship which now extends into almost every nation ... This great world fellowship is the great new fact of our era ... the one ground of hope for the coming days.'[9] And it is not possible to read the N.T. sensitively without feeling the power of its emphasis on the one Body or to continue to disregard the implication of: 'I in them, that they all may be one, as thou, Father, art in me and I in thee; that they also may be one in us; *that the world may believe that* thou has sent me.'[10]

Moreover, English Christians must look beyond the national boundary, not only northwards but to all parts of the world. How much the slowness of the progress towards unity and peace in Europe and the rest of the world is due to the disunity of the Church one cannot say; but the very question gives impetus to the movement towards reunion and prevents it from being too domestic and churchy. Reunion is not an attempt to build a Maginot line to save the Church 'from the godless man of modernity', but a resolve to renew its life and unity in Christ in order that it may be an effective instrument of God's activity throughout the world.

The problem of reunion is less one of 'orders' as one of achieving a unity that is at once there for men to see and is at the same time so spacious and free as to allow and encourage a rich variety in worship and life. This demands not so much theological agreement as more prayer and love, from bottom to top and top to bottom, deeply and sacramentally in Christ. It also demands of those who are guiding the several churches towards reunion a high quality of statesmanship fired by a prophetic vision which will enable them to hear what the Holy Spirit is saying to the churches from outside through scientists and artists, philosophers and social and industrial planners, as well as through new and corporate ventures in Christian living and mission where the Spirit is plainly at work.

3 'Spiritual and Material'

It is well, perhaps, that Christian theology did not fully think out its belief about the activity of the Divine Spirit in life before science lifted man's sights and gave him a new insight into and a fuller understanding of space and time and of the stuff of the universe. The scientific revolution and revelation have been, surely, the work of the Spirit. There is one recurring note in the New Testament to which the scientific mind is likely to be more sympathetic than an inelastic and rigid traditionalism has been. Nothing is more characteristic of the Gospel than faith in 'a God who comes', and its trust in the continuing ministry of the Spirit to lead men to truer knowledge and to give them courage to press beyond the old frontiers. This ministry is not isolated and individualist; men have to make this venture *together*, thereby ensuring its greater and more rapid success.

Christian faith thrives like science on uncertainties as well as on certainties. It is not afraid to recognize and to rejoice that the Divine Spirit operates through unsuspected agencies and outside the ecclesiastical terrain. 'The Spirit blows where it lists', said St John; and it is not always where theologians – or scientists or poets – expect him to go, or where ecclesiastical statesmen wish him to go. The idea that erring men might find a way of canalizing the activity of the Spirit of truth, wisdom and love so as to ensure the inerrancy of their choices and decisions is shown by history, even more than by argument, to be a fond and foolish, though persisting, delusion. It has been responsible for pogroms and persecutions, burnings and torture, and for making devout men claim the sanctions of the divine will for these crimes.

Not every wind that blows in God's world, of course, is the Spirit of love and truth. The corporate experience of the fellowship of the Spirit must always be a touchstone whether or not new currents of thought and life are of God or not. They are ultimately to be judged by their fruits (as in science by their congruity with the whole of knowledge). Time will show what argument cannot always prove. In the words of Oliver Quick, 'The Church's most searching critic will always be the Spirit whom Jesus gave to be her inward guide and interpreter of himself.' So in regard to criticism of traditional beliefs within herself or of new ideas impinging from outside, 'the Spirit operating in the whole body will prove its truth or falsehood when patience has done its perfect work'.[11]

In his presidential address to the British Association in 1964, Lord Brain was reported as saying that 'the greatest need of today is to acquire the power of looking ahead, forecasting and preparing for the consequences of the accelerating developments in science and technology'. He went on to say that the important division between people was not between the classical and scientific outlook on life, but between those who had been educated to see the world in terms of the rapidly changing environment which science was creating, with all its potentialities, and those who saw it in terms of the static environment and frozen emotional attitudes of the past. The first group had to educate the second, 'which includes many of our rulers ... we must prepare people for a new world which will be quite unlike the old'.[12]

Organized Christianity, far from cooperating in this campaign, has hitherto been resistant to this new outlook on life. Its more intelligent exponents have slowly come to accept the evolutionary hypothesis as fact, but the lines of communication between the new laboratories with their successful corporate experimentation and the theological colleges of the churches as yet hardly exist. It is superficially a matter of language – the difference between the classical tradition and the scientific. The language of poetry and the arts, and still more of liturgy belongs to the classical tradition – music alone is shared by the two cultures. Language changes only slowly with the changes in social culture; and so liturgy can only change slowly.

The difficulty and the difference is deeper, however, than linguistic. It has been an un-providential misfortune in the recent development of Christian thought that in the years between the wars when scientific developments were accelerating 'the Protestant world enthroned Barth while the Vatican exiled and did its best to silence Teilhard de Chardin.'[13]

The Roman Church never condemned Teilhard who was a deeply spiritual and obedient member of the Society of Jesus; but it did not allow him to publish his books. These have only been published since his death. He had to think out alone his synthesis between Christian orthodoxy and the fact of an evolutionary cosmos, in both of which he believed, and to invent his own terminology in which to expound his new insights. He had not even the advantage of discussion with the thinkers in this and other countries who were also developing ideas of creative evolution. Teilhard as an expert paleontologist who had given himself to exploring the traces of prehistoric man on and in the earth was convinced of the truth of evolution. He was also convinced that this is a psychosomatic universe and that 'the figure of the Christ as realized concretely in Christian experience is the most perfect representation of a final and complete objective that the universal effort of mankind can attain'.[14] The growing point, he believed, in the life of men is that they should be 'in Christ', not in a narrowly pietistic or moralistic sense, but in terms of that vision of the cosmic Christ which inspired and dominated St Paul in the full maturity of his thought.[15] Christ not only 'the Jesus of history', not only the creative word and the

Redeemer who overcame evil and death, but the consummation of the whole creative process.

If this interpretation of life and the universe towards which Teilhard was confidently feeling his way, and this warm acceptance of the revelations of science are together the line along which Christian thought will move in the next era, then some of the traditional language of Christian liturgy, with its emphasis on two worlds and two natures, will no longer serve the truth. The universe is a unity; the divide between body and mind, spiritual and material is not a sharply cut line. Evil remains a mysterious reality, preventing the true evolution and development of life; as it also hurts and maims human individuals and groups in their thinking and living; but the evolving cosmos is of God.

> The purity of beings is measured by the degree of the attraction that draws them towards the divine centre or, what comes to the same thing, by their nearness to the centre.[16]

A century ago F. D. Maurice, already quoted in this book, repudiated a sharp distinction between spiritual and secular, and the equation of spiritual with ecclesiastical and secular with the state which is thought by some to follow from it. Neither the life of men or society can be dissected so neatly. As F. von Hugel, the great Catholic philosopher in the early part of this century, used to say, the spiritual is known and interprets itself through the secular or material. Teilhard was reaching towards a finer synthesis and trying to build a bridge on which to walk carefully between science and faith – the synthesis which the future well-being of human society requires.

To those who are worried by this kind of re-thinking of traditional beliefs or by the argument developed by Bishop Wickham later in this book the following words by Quick who understood the spirituality of the Christian faith may brin g reassurance:

> The fact that Christianity is always its own severest critic is one proof that it is indeed the final and perfect religion for mankind.

And the way for the Church to keep and manifest her divinely ordained authority in faith is not to adopt measures of repression whenever the critic's voice is raised, but rather to trust the one Spirit to reconcile within the freedom of his own fellowship the diverse gifts of which he is the author.[17]

It may seem that one has moved a long way in this chapter from the title of this book, or even from the quotations in the introduction. Not so in reality. The new look of the Church must look out on reality and look forward to the new era that is arriving. A discussion of the Church–State relationship and of the inter-penetration of Church and national life must be set in this wider context and be related to these deeper issues if it is not to be trivial and ephemeral.

Given this changing society and the paramount need for a prophetic word that unifies the powers that are moulding its life, Christians and churchmen should wish to preserve and adapt to modern uses those lines of communication, opportunities for free dialogue and engagement, and the social contacts that have composed the inheritance of the Church of England. Once thrown away they cannot easily be recovered – certainly not in the lifetime of even the youngest of us.

NOTES

7. C. H. Smyth, *Church and Parish*, p. 33. Studies in Church problems illustrated from the parochial history of St Margaret's, Westminster, S.P.C.K.; being the Bishop Paddock Lectures in New York, 1953-4.

8. *Crown Appointments and the Church*, a report of a Commission appointed by the Archbishops, published November, 1964, by the Church Information Board. In appendices it prints: (i) A summary of Church and State relations in Scotland. (ii) An abstract (put into modern English) of the Annates Act of 1584 and Max Warren, *The Functions of a National Church*. (Epworth Press, 1964) cf. also *Scandinavian Churches*, Faber and Faber, 1965.

9. The sermon is printed in full in his collection of addresses, *The Church Looks Forward*, 1944.

10. St John's Gospel, Ch. 17, 21 & 23.

11. Oliver C. Quick (Regius Professor of Divinity at Durham and then

Oxford till he died in 1944). *The Doctrine of the Creeds*. Nisbet, 1938, pp. 303 & 323.

12. *The Times*, 27 August 1964, quoted in an article entitled *Thinking Ahead for a New World*, by their Special Correspondent, at the Southampton meeting of the British Association for the Advancement of Science.

13. *Teilhard de Chardin: Scientist and Seer*, by Charles E. Raven, Collins 1962, p. 29. A remarkable book for the Christian apologist to write at the end of his life in his seventy-ninth year.

14. ibid., p. 90. This is the theme of Teilhard's *Le Milieu Divin*, cf. also *The Phenomenon of Man*, pp. 292–9 and *The Hymn of the Universe*.

15. Epistles to the Ephesians, especially chapter 1, vv 3–23, and chapter 3, vv 9–21; to the Colossians, especially chapter 1, vv 12–20; and more applied to a man's thinking and living in the Epistle to the Philippians.

16. Teilhard de Chardin, *Le Milieu Divin*, English translation, p. 124.

17. Quick, ibid., p. 322.

'CHURCH AND STATE'
IN THE BIBLE

Introduction

THE purpose of this book is to re-examine the relation between Church and State. The purpose of this chapter is to
see what guidance we can get from the Bible on the subject.
In the Bible's own view, God works in history; so guidance
must come less from generalizations and isolated texts than
from seeing what happened.

To make the argument easier to follow, here is a summary:
(i) The Bible is concerned with the whole of life, not only
with religion. (ii) In the earliest times there is no distinction
between the religious and the secular; the religion of a community includes its whole ethos and outlook. (iii) The demands of the LORD as interpreted by the prophets cut across
the traditional ethos and outlook which Israel shared with
other nations, and set up a conflict and tension between them.
(iv) Other nations might adopt a secular outlook and adapt
religion to that; the LORD was too powerful for this to happen in Israel. (v) Government by prophets, by kings ruling
in the name of God, or by priests, was tried at various times,
but none succeeded in bringing political power under the rule
of the holy God and keeping it there. The nation called to
be holy never became a holy state. (vi) After the Exile in
Babylon and the Dispersion of many Jews in other places,
the nation was half way to becoming a church. (vii) In the
time of Christ Judaism was still 'established', and the problem
of finding a political expression for the holy community was
still unsolved. (viii) Our Lord by his death at the hands of the
Establishment completed the separation of the kingdom of
God from the kingdom of the world, and brought into being
the Christian Church based wholly on faith and obedience.

(ix) The Church had to produce an articulate structure of authority for itself, and to come to terms with the secular authority of Caesar. In taking its stand in the first place on a purely religious issue it was faithful to the implication of the whole biblical story. How it reinvaded the world, and the various compromises and adjustments which it was led to make, is the subject of other chapters.

The purpose of this chapter is to maintain that the distinction between the sacred and the secular, between duty to God and duty to the authorities of this world, was necessary and providential. The Church can never be identified with the British or any other nation at prayer, nor with any pattern of human culture. It has a mission to the whole world, but it can only fulfil that if the ground of its faith and authority is not in this world at all. Whether that means that here and now, or in any other time and place it must accept the position of a persecuted or a tolerated sect or set of sects, or can sit in council with the powers that be, depends upon contingent and varying factors.

(i) In the University Church at Oxford, on 14 July 1835, John Keble preached the sermon on 'National Apostasy', which John Henry Newman ever after regarded as marking the start of the Oxford Movement. He took as his text 1 Samuel, xii, 23: 'God forbid that I should sin against the LORD in ceasing to pray for you; but I will teach you the good and the right way.' The occasion of the sermon was the abolition by Parliament of certain Irish bishoprics; the occasion of Samuel's words was the insistence of the people on having a king like other nations, of which (according to this section of the Book of Samuel) the LORD by Samuel's mouth violently disapproved.[1] Keble was correct in seeing in this incident the first foreshadowing of a conflict, even of a division, between 'Church' and 'State'.

The words are in inverted commas, because to use any such terms of early communities and their religious institutions is to commit a gross anachronism. Even to use the word 'early' of the time of Samuel and Saul is a mistake. What we call early was already far advanced; the human race and its patterns of behaviour were already inconceivably old, and we can have only the dimmest clues to what the earliest communities were like in the relatively primitive ones which have survived into historical times.

'In the beginning' then, and for long after, we must suppose, art, ceremonial, ritual and moral traditions, etiquette, good manners (how you address your senior and junior relatives, and who takes precedence of whom, who can talk and who covers his lips), pastoral and agricultural techniques, are all part of a vast complex which covers the whole of life. Religion is not a separate activity. All these things together make it up. There are of course special occasions such as birth, marriage, death, seedtime and harvest, and war, which are particularly 'numinous', and to which special observances attach. But there is no hard and fast line between the religious and the secular, between the natural and the supernatural. Man and the world around him participate in one another and depend upon an order of which only a part is seen, and whose working is everywhere mysterious. In particular the fertility of man, of the beasts which he hunts or domesticates, and of the crops which he grows, depends upon maintaining a proper relation with the unseen powers. Offences against the code, which may be very detailed, particularly offences in sexual matters, endanger the whole community, and can only be atoned for by casting out the offender – often together with the people and things which are closely associated with him.

The unity of the tribe is maintained from generation to generation by the myths about the ancestors, how they came to the land they now possess (or how they had their origin there) and how they account for their particular customs. In many cases it is clear that the customs were there first, and the stories which were told to account for them came long afterwards. In these ancestral tales the first ancestors are usually semi-divine beings, and the account of how they came to this land which they now possess, or how they first came into being where they now are, merges into myths of the creation.

(ii) The integral, and in this sense primitive, community, maintains its distinctiveness from its neighbours in all these ways, and is sensitively aware of the various degrees of closeness and remoteness in which it stands to them. Dorians and Ionians, Lacedemonians and Athenians are all Hellenes, while others are barbarians. Israel and Edom are cousins, while Philistines are foreigners to both. This is symbolized by descent from common ancestors who personify a real racial and cultural fact.

The guardians of the tradition are the elders, both men and women, supplemented by specially gifted story-tellers and singers, and an essential part of initiation into full membership at puberty is the learning of the tradition.

Identifiable 'states' as distinct from tribes or groups of tribes, apparently emerge when military conquest brings people of different origins under one rule, or where, as in the city states of the Mediterranean area, a common place of residence becomes more important than a common origin. Even so the state is not a 'secular' organization, the myths are merged and adjusted to one another by conquest and assimilation, and the gods and heroes are given a local habitation. The king is not only commander in war, and ruler, but a visible link between his people and the powers above. He is often himself descended from the gods.

All this could be illustrated from the legends of Greece and Rome, in both of which clear traces of the earlier outlook survived into classical times. The heroes who gave their names to peoples and regions were descended from the gods; both athletic contests and the drama were religious observances, and the title *Basileus* or *Rex* continued to be used for religious functionaries when the political and military duties of the king had long ago been taken over by others. The 'Aryan', Olympian, official gods had associated with them dark companions which belonged to the older religions of the land, and which had been conquered but not abolished by the invaders. The same is true of India, where Hinduism has preserved to the present day an all-inclusive permeation of life by religion, and where religion itself has shown, in a degree unparalleled elsewhere, a capacity for including all sorts of apparently incompatible elements absorbed from the different races which now inhabit the land.

Nor is the Bible, to start with, an exception. The people who came to know themselves as Israelites started as a collection of tribes who shared the background of their neighbours and many of their customs and stories. Circumcision[2] was far older than Abraham, and the Feast of Unleavened Bread[3] than the Exodus. Religion, for them as for their neighbours, was an all-embracing frame of reference which governed every activity and every part of life. They did not distinguish, as we are inclined to do, between ritual and hygienic purity, nor, at the beginning, moral purity from either. The LORD* was their God, much as Chemosh was the God of Moab,[4] and Moloch of Ammon. Their battles were his battles, and his victories were theirs. There are in fact close parallels between the language in which the king of Moab attributes his successes to Chemosh and the language of the Psalms.

(iii) What made them in the end so different from their neighbours? They themselves continually pointed to Moses and the Exodus. In the vision of the Burning Bush[5] the LORD had revealed his Name, and summoned his people from Egyptian slavery. He was not bound to them by natural ties as the gods of the other nations were, but of his own free will had chosen them, called them to be holy,[6] and given them the Law. When

---

* I am following the custom of the AV and RV in substituting the LORD (in capitals) for the Name of YHWH, which was too holy to be pronounced, and for which the Jews substitute Adonai (LORD) when speaking. 'Jehovah' is a barbarous combination of the consonants of one with the vowels of the other.

they eventually entered the Promised Land they were joined by other tribes (if modern scholars are right) who had not actually been in Egypt, but who had their own experiences of deliverance (as from Sisera by Deborah and Barak).[7] They too became members of the LORD's peculiar people, and in the annual repetition of the Passover sacrifice,[8] through song and dance ('The Lord hath triumphed gloriously: the horse and his rider hath he thrown into the sea'), they knew that they belonged together so that what was done through Moses had been done for them as well. The historical books and many of the Psalms make articulate the 'myth' of Israel's origin and calling which explained why they were different, dedicated, a holy people. In the light of this they reinterpreted the legends of the Patriarchs, and saw in them the hand of the same LORD working already in the distant past.

(iv) The prophets established, not without difficulty, what perhaps was implicit already in the message of Moses, the distinction between moral and ceremonial purity, and seem at times to be indifferent to the outward forms of religious observance. 'I hate, I despise your feast days, and I will not smell in your solemn assemblies ... but let judgment run down as waters, and righteousness as a mighty stream'.[9] This will become the basic mark of holiness, for the holy God is of purer eyes than to behold iniquity.

The LORD was a jealous God,[10] who would tolerate no rival. To be holy meant to be different, separate, and to belong to him alone. The land which they conquered was to be holy too.[11] The customs of their neighbours were an offence to him, and their idols fit only for destruction. The LORD himself was high and holy,[12] as Creator he made the heaven and the earth, he sent the rain and caused the sun to shine, and gave good crops, and made Israel's wives to be joyful mothers of children. But he was not *in* these things, and the sexual licence which elsewhere was a means of ensuring fertility was a degradation of his honour.

The constant danger was re-infection of Israel's religion from outside. In fact we shall better understand the destruction of Achan[13] with his wife and children and all that he possessed, by our own attitude to infection than by our own ideas of justice. For Jericho, a corrupt and luxurious city by all accounts, had been declared accursed, and by taking a wedge of gold and a Babylonish garment and hiding them in the floor of his tent, Achan had endangered the whole people. Similarly when Saul had saved the best of the spoil from the doomed Amalekites 'to sacrifice unto the LORD in Gilgal',[14] as he said, we shall understand Samuel's condemnation of Saul if we think of a nurse who against the doctor's orders has omitted to burn the clothes of a patient who has died of smallpox.

(v) Can the holy nation be a holy state? This is the question with which we are concerned. Can it be a state, with all the apparatus of statehood, and still be holy? In the view taken by Samuel according to the section of 1 Samuel we have already quoted,[15] it could not. The only proper form of government for a holy people was theocracy, the direct rule of God as represented by his prophets and priests, as in the time of Moses and Aaron. But according to the account given in the other chapters, the LORD himself appointed Saul to save his people from the Philistines.[16] The scholars explain the discrepancy by pointing out that some of the things with which Samuel is said to have threatened the people as the result of having a king reflect the experience and disillusionment of a later age.[17] But there is more to it than that. Samuel very soon fell out with Saul when he found he was not going to be an obedient tool. At the very beginning of his reign, before fighting his first battle against the Philistine conquerors, Saul had waited for Samuel to perform the preliminary sacrifice, beyond the appointed time;[18] and when Samuel was late for his appointment, and the army which he had gathered together had already begun to fade away, Saul took upon himself to perform the sacrifice instead. Samuel was deeply offended, and told him that he had forfeited the kingdom. Not only this, but he secretly anointed David,[19] who in the course of time was inevitably driven into revolt.

In fact the kingdom of David, where the holy nation was ruled by the LORD's anointed king, became the first and most fully articulated image of what a holy nation ought to be. It never ceased to haunt their imagination; it was this kind of picture which the Apostles had in mind when they asked our Lord 'Wilt thou at this time restore the kingdom to Israel?'[20] And 'Solomon in all his glory'[21] ever after appealed to them as a picture of the glory which once had been theirs, in spite of the very frank admission of the dubious means by which he had maintained it.[22]

There could still be no simple division between the 'sacred' and the 'secular'. The king represented his people to God, and ruled by divine right. David's own reverence for Saul ('for who shall stretch forth his hand against the LORD's anointed, and be guiltless?')[23] illustrated the point. Many of the Psalms, e.g. 24, 45 and 72, reflect this belief, and we can imagine Ps. 24 and others being sung as the king makes a ceremonial entrance into the holy city, to take possession of his inheritance in the name of the LORD.

(vi) But where did the seat of ultimate authority lie – with the king, or with the prophet? Many peoples, of whom the Romans are the most familiar instance, kept prophets of a sort, soothsayers, astrologers, augurs and such, to read the omens, study the disposition of the stars, forecast the results of various lines of action, and give advice accordingly. Ahab's prophets,[24] who advised him with one voice to go up to Ramoth-Gilead and prosper, may have been little more. But Micaiah son of Imlah, who told Ahab the truth, spoke with a different and authoritative voice, and roundly declared that the LORD had put a lying spirit[25] in the mouth of all the other prophets.

The 'still small voice'[26] which Elijah heard on the holy mountain told him to inaugurate two violent revolutions, which he did by the agency of Elisha. The two greatest prophets, Isaiah and Jeremiah, were continually 'interfering in politics'. When Isaiah said, 'In quietness and confidence shall be your strength',[27] he meant that Hezekiah, who was a tributory of Assyria, should not intrigue with Egypt with a view to revolt. When later the Babylonians were besieging the city, and Jeremiah[28] was spreading alarm and despondency, threatening the king and advising surrender, he came very near to treason. It is no surprise to learn[29] that when there was a let up in the siege and he was seen going off into the country the princes said he was deserting to the enemy and put him in prison; nor that when the city fell he was released and rewarded by the King of Babylon.[30]

If this first attempt to realize the kingdom of God on earth which was also to be an actual kingdom failed, it is because it attempted to do what the other nations never even attempted. But in the course of the failure the vision and the hope took wing. In promising that if they kept the LORD's commandments the people should live securely, every man under his vine and fig-tree,[31] the prophets were disappointed. But the vision they had seen expanded into the vision of a world at peace. The God who had dealt so hardly with his people became the only God of all the world. Jerusalem and the kingdom of David came to stand for a kingdom which David's kingdom never was, Jerusalem for the city that has foundations, whose builder and maker is God.[32]

(vii) The effect of the exile was to make the issues clearer. There were some who inferred that if trying to serve the LORD had brought them to this, it did not pay, and the sensible thing was to try the Queen of Heaven[33] or other gods and goddesses who might be more effective – who *were* more effective, judged by the success of their followers. Of those who went away, and of their descendants, only a few[34] an-

swered the call to return to ruined Jerusalem and rebuild her
temple and her walls. The bond which held them was a
religious one. Now more than ever they must protect themselves and their faith against the contaminations of the
heathen. Ezra[35] and Nehemiah laid great stress on the rebuild-
ing of the Temple and on the meticulous observance of the
sacrificial offerings. They successfully resisted the attempts of
the local inhabitants to interfere with them,[36] but also rejected
their proferred help,[37] and compelled the people to put away
their foreign wives.[38] This school of thought was responsible
for the re-writing of the national story, notably in I and II
Chronicles, but also in a number of other passages in the
earlier books. The stress is on the importance of meticulous
obedience and this was rewarded by miraculous interventions
of the LORD.[39] It is a thoroughly 'clerical' view of history, and
indicates the kind of approach to political questions which
priests might be expected to adopt.

To the priestly influence of Ezra the scribe and his successors may be traced the narrow orthodox Judaism which is so
prominent in the New Testament. Its strength and toughness
is shown by the fact that it kept the people to their faith even
when they were subject to a succession of heathen rulers, and
when a normal inference from the facts might well be that the
LORD was powerless.

For the greater part of the time the peculiar observances of
the Jews were tolerated by their rulers. But when Antiochus
Epiphanes[40] in 168 B.C. having spoiled the Temple forbade
them to observe the Law and attempted to compel them to
sacrifice to idols they were goaded into revolt and, led by the
Maccabees, won their independence. Jerusalem became once
more the capital of a state, and for most of the next 80 years
was independent;[41] ruled by High Priests, for the most part
connected with the Maccabean family, who added to the
priesthood the royal title. But it was a dismal period. Generally,
the priest kings were no better than the petty rulers of the
neighbouring states. They murdered their own relatives to
secure the throne, they massacred and intrigued, and laid

waste the country round, now driving out Greeks for being Greeks, now admitting Greek customs into Jerusalem and giving themselves Greek names.

If the spirit of Judaism survived all this it was perhaps due to the Pharisees and the Rabbis, who delighted in the Law and put their main hope outside this world altogether. The LORD would vindicate his faithful in the resurrection from the dead even though this world was full of wickedness and violence.

But the Judaism of Palestine represents only half the story, numerically the smaller half. In Egypt, Mesopotamia, and eventually throughout the Roman Empire settlements of Jews were scattered – the Jews of the 'Dispersion'. Temple worship and sacrifice were denied to them (though one 'High Priest' set up a 'Temple' in Egypt). The reading of the Scriptures in the synagogue, and the worship centred in the Scriptures, their dietary rules and circumcision, marked them off from their neighbours and kept them in the faith (as indeed it has done till the present day), and made them still a peculiar people. The scholars who translated the Old Testament into Greek lived in Alexandria in Egypt, as did Philo, who linked up the faith of the Bible with Greek philosophy. Jerusalem was still the centre and the place of pilgrimage (rather as Mecca is for the Muslims), but the majority of Jews lived elsewhere. The practice of their religion was independent of what might be happening in the mother city, and survived its destruction.

Thus the period between the testaments would seem to show that the direct rule by ecclesiastics is not the answer. They too are corrupted by power, and the more nearly absolute their power becomes, the more they are corrupted. But true religion can flourish in foreign lands and under alien governments.

When Rome had restored some sort of order to the world, and the half-foreign Herod had been installed as king of a vassal state, religion was still 'established'. Herod the Great, though a merciless tyrant, rebuilt the Temple on a more magnificent scale, the High Priest was a man of power and influence, the Sanhedrin had authority to punish, though not with death, and Jerusalem was kept clear of images. This was continued when Judaea some years after Herod's death came under the direct rule of Rome.

In this situation 'the Church' in Palestine was still in part the nation in its religious aspect, so that the powers remaining to its authorities were more than those belonging to a voluntary society or sect which has never been other than that. Thus the Messianic title (Christ) had political overtones, ecclesiastical parties were directly involved in political questions, and disputes about religious doctrine raised political issues. The Sadducees wanted a decent conformity to the main traditional customs; they were a 'Whiggish' compromising party, who did not want to disturb the equilibrium by being too particular. They did not expect or want anything to change very much. The position of the Herodians was similar. The Pharisees found foreign domination much more irksome, and kept alive the hope that if the people would return to their true obedience the LORD would once more set his people free, and vindicate them in the eyes of all the nations as the people whom the LORD had chosen for his own. They did not commit themselves to the way of armed revolt, but many of those who worked underground for that must have been inspired by their zeal. The two parties combined to demand the crucifixion of our Lord. The Pharisees wanted it because he was endangering the purity of the holy people by his loose attitude to the Law and the encouragement that he gave to the publicans and sinners. The Sadducees wanted it because any enthusiastic revival of religious hopes might upset the *status quo*. Pilate yielded to their demand because his own position was not too safe, and he could not afford to have the Jews united against him in saying 'Thou art not Caesar's friend'.[43]

In effect the Establishment on both its sides, the foreign government which recognized it, and the religious authorities who represented it, combined to destroy the One in whom, had they known it, the destiny of Israel was being fulfilled.

(viii) The Church which the Spirit of the risen Christ brought into being on the Day of Pentecost[43] had no recognized standing at all. It appeared to be a heretical sect within Judaism, and as such was tolerated by the Romans. Gallio, who 'cared for none of these things', was not even much troubled when different sorts of Jews were beating one another.[44] The Town Clerk of Ephesus[45] was only concerned with maintaining public peace. St Paul was arrested in Jerusalem under the impression that he was a violent revolutionary,[46] and when it was discovered that he was in trouble only because of matters of Jewish doctrine and observance, he might have been set at liberty if he had not appealed to Caesar.[47]

The fact that he did appeal to Caesar shows that he recognized the authority of Caesar in his own department, and claimed his rights as a Roman citizen,[48] not to be punished except for an overt breach of the law of the state. The exhortations to civil obedience in his Epistles and in I Peter go no further than this.[49]

The difficult saying of Christ, 'Render unto Caesar the things that are Caesar's, and unto God the things that are God's'[50] is probably to be interpreted in a similar sense. The Lord was not going to encourage rebellion, but neither was he allowing that Caesar had any power in determining matters of religious obedience.

When the Apostles said, 'We must obey God rather than men'[51] they were addressing the established authorities of the religion in which they had been brought up. When later on the Christians refused to give worship to Caesar they were defying the authority of the state.

Finally, in the Book of Revelation, Rome appears as Babylon the great,[52] doomed to destruction as the enemy of God and his saints.

It would not be true to say that our Lord was indifferent to the affairs of this world. His parables show a realistic and even genial appreciation of ordinary human nature. The farmers, tradesmen, parents and children, employers and workers who appear in his parables are not idealized. The man who knows there is treasure buried in the corner of a field[53] buys the field without mentioning to the owner that the treasure is there. The father who opens his door to the friend who knocks at midnight does so rather than be kept any longer awake.[54] The master who expects his servant, after working all day in the field, to serve him at supper before he has his own[55] – these are people as they are, and not as they ought to be. The crops and the buildings well or badly founded behave as crops and buildings everywhere may be expected to do. But, as has often been pointed out, in his teaching of his own disciples he shows no interest in the relativities and compromises by which alone civic order can be maintained.

'Give to every one that asketh thee; and of him that taketh away thy goods ask them not again.'[56] 'Lay not up for yourselves treasures upon the earth, where moth and rust consume, and where thieves break through and steal.'[57] 'If any man would go to law with thee, and take away thy coat, let him have thy cloak also.'[58] 'Be not anxious saying, What shall we eat? or, What shall we drink? or, Wherewithal shall we be clothed? Behold the birds of the air, that they sow not, neither do they reap, nor gather into barns; and your heavenly Father feedeth them.'[59] Taken as literal prescriptions for behaviour these and similar sayings would mean the end of commerce and the enforcement of law; there would be no accummulations of capital, no provision for the future. These things are the rightful concern of the secular authorities, but his kingdom is not of this world.[60]

(ix) It might seem from the above reading of the biblical story, that the logical conclusion would be something like the Qumran Community, entirely withdrawn from the world, looking for a deliverance which was to be entirely supernatural. For a time they did live in the immediate expectation of the End. Writing to the Thessalonians, St Paul assured them that those who had died would be at no disadvantage compared with himself and his correspondents, who, he takes for granted, will be alive at the coming of the Lord.[61] Some of his advice in matters of sex was affected by this expectation.[62]

If the Lord had given to the Church a detailed constitution or a list of rules, it might have remained an enclosed sect literally till Doomsday. Actually, he gave it no mandate except to witness, and no equipment but what his Spirit gave,[63] and the memory of his words and acts. But the mandate to bear witness, and the Spirit which drove his followers out ensured that the re-invasion of the world should begin. The very fact that they had no detailed programme, and that the vista of an indefinite future was obscured by the picture of final judgement ensured that no first century, second century... no pattern of any century obedience should be imprinted on the Church for all time to come.

The process of reintegration began at ground level because there was no other. Not many wise after the flesh, not many mighty, not many noble, were called.[64] The primitive communism of the Jerusalem church in its early days[65] did not endure, and seems never to have been other than voluntary.[66] But giving it up must have felt like the beginning of compromise with the ways of the world.

Far more serious was the readjustment when the Church broke out of the narrow limits of Judaism into the Gentile world. Much to his surprise St Peter discovered that the Spirit could be given to a Roman who had not been made a Jew.[67] This followed a vision of which the details may well have been suggested by the port of Joppa with its sailing boats trading with all parts of the world. But it was St Paul who in this issue fought the greatest battle of his life, and after convicting even St Peter of backsliding secured[68] for all time the right of the Gentiles to enter the Church without having to keep the details of the Jewish law. For him anything else would have been a reversion to the self-preserving, self-justifying idea of holiness which had caused the crucifixion of the Lord, and had misled him into persecuting the Lord's disciples.

For the rest, the simple ethical rules, taken over largely

from the Pharisees, and repeated in epistle after epistle,[69] in what we have been taught to describe as the primitive catechism – civil obedience, the relations of husbands and wives, parents and children, masters and slaves, the natural human everyday dealings of people with one another – these are the very places in which the gifts of the Spirit are to manifest themselves. The fellowship of the holy Spirit is to be realized in all these humdrum ways. The supreme gift of the charity which never fails[70] is described in terms of people living together in a close-knit company. Nothing less than the whole self-giving of the Christ who humbled himself in becoming man and taking on himself the form of a servant, who was obedient even to the death of the cross – nothing less than this is brought to bear on the petty rivalries and one-upmanship of the Philippians.[71] So far from waiting about in idleness for the End the Christians are to earn their own living,[72] and to give to those in need. One of St Paul's first tasks is to organize a collection for inter-church aid.[73]

As it spreads and becomes more varied the Church has to produce an articulate pattern of authority within itself. The personal authority of the Apostles[74] will be supplemented and continued by an authority dependent on office.[75] The 'ministers' of the Church are the servants of Christ,[76] and it is perhaps for their sakes in particular that the Lord's sayings about authority based on service were remembered.[77] Overseers, elders and servants will become stereotyped as bishops, presbyters, and deacons, but this belongs to a later period.

We see already in the New Testament the beginning of adaptation to the necessities of persecution.[78] Only later will the contrary question of political power have to be faced, but the same principles will apply in a much more difficult testing.

St Paul had said to the Philippians 'Our citizenship is in heaven',[79] and they would understand very well what he meant. For Philippi itself was a Roman colony in Macedonia, situated in one place, but bound by loyalty to another. So the Christians belonged already to the kingdom which is not of this world, but this world was the place where the life of heaven was to be lived. They were, we might say, a bridgehead for the new way of life.

'Ye shall be holy, for I, the LORD, am holy'.[80] For a time this meant increasing separation, a breaking up of the primitive unity, in order that the Absolutely Holy should prepare for its own entry into a confused unholy world. That process reached its crisis when the Absolutely Holy was made man, and inaugurated the new pattern of holiness which does not fear contamination, which refuses to be protected, but exposes itself to the unholy and pays the cost of doing so. The Church which has his Spirit, or rather which his Spirit has and holds,[81] can afford to take risks and to be entangled in politics and commerce. It can continually touch pitch without being defiled; it can go into the darkest and murkiest places with a fire that consumes the evil and purifies the impure, with a light that darkness cannot overcome;[82] if it tries to save its life it loses it, if it spends itself it lives.

'In the end' the unity is to be restored. There will be no distinction between the secular and the sacred, where all is holy. But the unity is infinitely richer because of the distinctions which it now includes, and so the vision we are given of the end is not of a return to primitive life, but of a city, new Jerusalem,[83] descending from heaven 'and the nations shall walk in the light thereof; and the kings of the earth do bring their glory into it'[84] and 'the kingdom of the world is become the kingdom of our God and of his Christ, and he shall reign for ever and ever'.[85]

*

The vision still hides the distant future from our eyes, as it always has. At times the colony has felt like a beleaguered city, looking to its foundations and marking well its bulwarks. At other times in a more genial climate it has extended its territory – and sometimes has been in danger of assimilation to the world. These things belong to church history, and contingent and relative factors enter in.

Jesus said, '*Fear not, little flock, for it is your Father's good pleasure to give you the kingdom.*'

'*Woe unto you when all men speak well of you.*'

'*They which are accounted to rule over the Gentiles lord it over them; and their great ones exercise authority over them. But it is not so among you; but whosoever would become great among you shall be your servant; for verily the Son of man came not to be ministered unto, but to minister, and to give his life a ransom for many.*'[86]

BIBLICAL REFERENCES

1. Gen. xxxvi, 1–9; Amos i, 11; cf. Gen. xix. 30–8 (I hated Moab and Ammon).
2. Gen. xvii, 10.
3. Exod. xii, 39.
4. Judges xi, 23–4.
5. Exod. iii, 1–14.
6. Exod. xix, 6.
7. Judges iv and v.
8. Exod. xii, 27, and xv, 1.
9. Amos v, 21 and 24; cf. Isa. i, 13.
10. Exod. xx, 5.
11. Num. xxxv, 34; Lev. xviii, 24–30.
12. Isa. lvii, 15; cf. Isa. vi, 1–3.
13. Joshua vii.
14. 1 Sam. xv, 21.
15. 1 Sam. xii; cf. 1 Sam. vii, 13.
16. 1 Sam. ix, 16; x.
17. 1 Sam. viii, 10–18.
18. 1 Sam. xiii, 8–14.
19. 1 Sam. xvi, 1–13.
20. Acts i, 6.
21. Matt. vi, 29.
22. 1 Kings xi.
23. 1 Sam. xxvi, 9; cf. xxiv, 6.
24. 1 Kings xxii.
25. ibid. v. 22.
26. 1 Kings xix, 12; 11 Kings viii, 7–15; ix, 1–10.
27. Isa. xxx, 15.
28. e.g. Jer. xix; xxi, 1–10.
29. Jer. xxxvii, 11–15.
30. Jer. xl, 1–4.
31. 1 Kings iv, 25; Mic. iv, 4; Zech. iii, 10.
32. Heb. xi, 10.
33. Jer. xliv, 17.
34. e.g. Ezra viii, 1–14.
35. Ezra iii; cf. 1 Kings viii, esp. 63–4.
36. Nehemiah iv.
37. Ezra. iv, 1–3.
38. Ezra x.
39. 11 Chron. xiii, xiv, xx.
40. 1 Macc. i, 41.
41. For this period see e.g. Edwyn Bevan in Gore's S.P.C.K. Commentary.
42. John xix, 12.
43. Acts ii, 1.
44. Acts xviii, 17.
45. Acts xix, 35.
46. Acts xxi, 38.
47. Acts xxvi, 32.
48. Acts xxii, 28; xxv, 11.
49. Rom. xiii, 1–7; 1 Pet. ii, 13–17.
50. Mark xii, 13–17.
51. Acts v, 29.

52. Rev. xiv, 8.
53. Matt. xiii, 44.
54. Luke xi, 5–8.
55. Luke xvii, 7.
56. Luke vi, 30.
57. Matt. vi, 19.
58. Matt. v, 40.
59. Matt. vi, 26, 31.
60. John xviii, 36.
61. 1 Thess. iv, 15.
62. 1 Cor. vii, 29.
63. 1 Cor. xii; Eph. iv, 11.
64. 1 Cor. i, 26.
65. Acts iv, 32–7.
66. Acts v, 4.
67. Acts x.
68. Gal. ii, 11–14; iii, 1–3 and 13.
69. Eph. v, 22 seq; Col. iii, 12 seq.; 1 Pet. ii, 13 seq.
70. 1 Cor. xiii.
71. Phil. ii, 1–11.
72. 11 Thess. iii, 10; Eph. iv, 28.
73. Acts xi, 30; 11 Cor. ix; Rom. xv, 25–9.
74. 1 Cor. i etc; 11 Cor. x, 1–12.
75. Acts vi, 3; 11 Tim. i, 6; Titus i, 5.
76. 1 Cor. iv, 1; 1 Tim. i, 12; 1 Pet. v, 1–4.
77. Mark x, 42–5.
78. e.g. 1 Pet. iii, 13.
79. Phil. iii, 20.
80. Lev. xix, 2 etc.
81. Phil. iii, 12.
82. John i, 5; xii, 35–6; Eph. v, 13, etc.
83. Rev. xxi, 2.
84. Rev. xxi, 24.
85. Rev. xi, 15.
86. Luke xii, 32; Luke vi, 26; Mark x, 42.

'CHURCH AND STATE' IN
HISTORY – MAINLY ENGLISH

DISCUSSION of the national character of the Church of England, or the nature of its establishment, raises the general question of the relationship between Church and State.

It needs to be said at the outset that there is not, and in the nature of the case there cannot be, any one definitive connexion, because the character of neither is fixed: they are not 'entities' which exist in pure form; their purposes overlap and intertwine. Consequently their mutual relations are subtle, intricate and ever-changing. It is not surprising, therefore, that there are almost as many interpretations of the simple dominical injunction 'Render unto Caesar the things that are Caesar's, and to God the things that are God's' as there are interpreters.

The fact is that though this succinct dictum establishes a clear regulative principle, its application bristles with difficulty whenever it is introduced into particular situations. The practical problem of deciding conflicting loyalties is not usually one of determining priorities, which in principle are often transparently clear. Obviously the claims of God's Kingdom must take precedence over the kingdoms of men. In the concrete, the real difficulty – and it can be agonizing – is to determine what is of God and what is of Caesar. 'Fear God and honour the King' seeks to combine both loyalties, but often, as in Nazi Germany for example, Christians have felt that this was impossible and they have been forced to give up the struggle.

The relation of Church to State is, I repeat, both complex and difficult. In particular situations the determinative factor concerning their mutual confrontation can be put in the form of a question: What kind of Church; and what kind of State?

Christianity is not primarily a philosophical system, a

'gnosis', commitment to which has no very obvious repercussions on society. It is a way of life, constraining the whole
man in his total or existential situation. There is no private
world – or ought not to be – to which a Christian dedication
is alien; no inner sanctuary of the soul where the claims of
faith may not penetrate.

And this way of life takes account of, and is concerned with,
that wider community which is essential to man's development: and it sees this community not simply as the necessary
embryo in which the individual person is born, but as a
historic, changing and therefore developing society moving
towards an end.

Christianity is a historical faith in a double sense. Not only
was it born in history; but it took its rise from certain 'events'
which were interpreted as having unique significance, since
through them 'God was working His purpose out as year
succeeded to year'. Such a view of Christian faith might seem
to lead to a theocracy, such as the Jews, as well as Calvin,
sought after in their concept of a holy nation; that is, a nation
in which law, government, even foreign policy are expressions
of the divine will. But apart from the fact that theocracies do
not seem to work and easily degenerate into tyrannies, it is,
for the modern Christian, idle to speculate upon this form of
government. Some Communist states may succeed for the
time being, at least, in establishing a theocracy without God;
yet the general drift in contemporary Europe is towards a
secular if not always a liberal society. This drift can be
recognized in some recent pronouncements of the Vatican
Council.

My concern in this chapter is with the role of the Church
of England in our national life, but before we enter upon such
a discussion it is important to ask one over-riding question:
'What is the primary task of the Christian Church?'

The answer is not difficult though the implications of the
answer are tremendous. The task is, surely, 'to give glory to
God by witnessing to and building his Kingdom, through
commitment to Jesus.' There is no room here to elaborate this

statement, except to say that this kingdom is a personal order, in which men fulfil themselves by entering into free, mature and sacrificial relations with each other. Christian belief as to the trinitarian nature of God, the Supreme Existent, roots this personal confrontation in the basic structure of reality. A truly personal order, for its realization here and now, demands the dimensions of space and time; and these are the essential 'stuff' of the historic process. It is right, therefore, for the Christian to see God as working to build his Kingdom within this continuum, in response to man's free committal.

Such a basic attitude to history, and its relevance to the personal and collective life, must be regarded as integral to a fully Christian 'ideology'. It supposes an attitude which is prepared to give reality to the flux and change of human affairs, but looks within and beyond them to a grand consummation in the Kingdom of God.

Yet such a more than cosmic view does not provide a blueprint of how this personal order, towards which history is to move, can be established in particular situations. True, the Church as the 'Body of Christ' sees itself as the agent, though not necessarily the only agent, through which the Kingdom is to be progressively built. As such, the ambition of the Church must be that its interior life should express that quality of sacrificial self-giving which the Kingdom is meant to embody. But the Church lives in the world and is necessarily caught up in the complexities and challenges which such involvement brings. Indeed it was launched upon its historic course within a great civilization, the Empire of Rome; and it was upon this Empire, and not upon the Church, that there lay the heavy responsibility for maintaining law and order, and for discharging the duties normally associated with government. The '*plenitudino potestatis*' rested in Caesar's hands. Whatever final judgement be made upon the achievements of Rome, few can deny their range and extent. Many of her statesmen, including some of her Emperors, had drunk deeply from the wells of Greek philosophy, and were themselves encouraged thereby to speculate upon the nature and purpose of government.

Such reflections as the above are immediately relevant to the relation of Church to State, since they make it clear that the situational context of the Christian community has varied from age to age. For this reason the problems which these differing environments have thrown up could not be solved by the logical application of a slick principle.

To St Paul many of the dilemmas which oppressed later and contemporary generations were unknown. He saw the churches which he founded in the Roman-Greek world as focal points or 'cells' of the Kingdom, from which believers, many of them of low social status, some even slaves, were to go out and live sacrificially in the wider world, taking what came to them. Inevitably Paul accepted the social forms of his day, but tried to breathe into them, within the Christian communities, charity and understanding. For example, it would have been ridiculous to campaign for a Christian foreign policy for the Roman Empire. Enough, for the time being, if these groups could lodge themselves perilously within the contemporary order. To exercise governmental influence, or to become a pressure group, was beyond Paul's wildest dreams. Indeed within a matter of years, the Church, under Nero, was being submitted to severe persecution and her very existence was in jeopardy.

Yet within some three centuries the relationship of the Christian Church to the State had changed. From being a minority group, largely recruited from among the underprivileged, it was now influential and well organized, so much so that Constantine decided to make Christianity the official religion of the Roman Empire. The result was the final shedding of an earlier pacifism, and an increasing involvement in the complex life of a great Empire in its overall governmental responsibilities. Christians now, by reason of their new status, were required to work out what it meant to build the Kingdom of God, that is to establish a truly personal order, in the more challenging and resistant contexts of the collective life. They had to relate their faith to the conduct of affairs at an imperial level, to dealing with the barbarian at the gate, and introducing the insights of faith, with their emphasis on compassion, into the effort to establish patterns of justice between man and man. In other words, they were called to witness to their Lord within a context of power.

The result, to the historian, may seem sadly disappointing, and it is understandable that a stock question in the schools is to ask whether Constantine's acceptance of Christianity did more to secularize the Church than it did to sanctify the State. Opinions vary: but there can be no doubt that Christians were right to accept the status which the Emperor offered them, though it is arguable that the accommodation which they made was at too low a level. They compromised overmuch. To have rejected the offer, however, would have been false to the whole historic tradition which the Church had inherited in its concept of a holy nation; and it would also have been an open recognition that Christian faith was irrelevant to the interests of the wider society in which men lived. Failure to measure up to the challenge would have weakened the hold of Christian faith on those whose responsibility it was to involve themselves in the day-to-day discharge of government.

This thumb-nail historic sketch is intended to show that though the overriding intention of the Church is always the same, it will set about this enduring task in different ways in response to the varying circumstances in which it finds itself. Sometimes the Christian Church is itself a contributory factor in moulding this environment: at others this environment is largely 'given', and must be accepted, at least for the time being. The relations into which the Church collectively – and its members individually – always concerned to build God's Kingdom – will enter with the State and with the surrounding society will vary according to whether these relations are worked out in Nero's Rome, in the Empire of Constantine, in medieval Europe, in contemporary Russia, America, Ghana, or India. In all these varying situations the

State is itself a different kind of entity and the Christian Church has contributed differently, across the years, to its collective life.

Also, in reverse, the Church, so far as the psychology of its members is concerned, is itself different in these diverse contexts, according to the response which it has made to cultural and political pressures. Moreover the attitude of the State may vary from glad acceptance to a tolerance which shades off into open hostility. This must evoke on the part of the Church correspondingly different reactions and these will affect its theological rationale. Also different Churches will have developed subtly diverse attitudes to involvement and withdrawal. One thing is certain. No Church can remain finally indifferent to what the State does to, and requires of, those 'who profess and call themselves Christians' – and, it is hoped, of citizens generally. Nearly all that the State tries to do has some relationship, remote or near, with the building up of a personal order.

So it is that the question which the Christian Church must always ask itself – 'What relations with the State, in so far as the Church is in a position to control such relations, will best help the discharge of its primary duty of building the Kingdom?' – will be answered in different ways. And these answers will not, except in respect of the principle that they presuppose, provide a blueprint for other Churches whose traditions, collective psychology and circumstances cannot be the same. The role of the Christian Church in India, for example, living as it does alongside resurgent older faiths and having been for two centuries the handmaid of an imperial power, cannot in its day-to-day expression be the same as that in a liberal state in Western Europe. True, involvement must be a common duty, but this will constrain a variety of responses.

It is, therefore, a commonplace to assert that our own English scene is unique. So are the Spanish, the French, the German and the Russian, to mention only a few. Of course, these situations have a great deal in common, for all the above nations have reaped something from the rich harvest of Western Europe: but they have done this in different ways.

My concern, in the rest of this chapter, is with the scene which we know best in the England of the twentieth century: and my basic contention here is that if we are to be sensitive to what is happening around us, and are prepared to ask the right questions, then we must know something of the particular history which has brought us to our present situation. We shall not get very far if our only questions are the theoretically logical ones: 'What is, or ought to be, the normative relation between Church and State? What are their different "ends", in so far as they are different? And how in their relations with each other can they, by mutual interaction, promote them?'

Of course we cannot deny, as Aristotle wisely affirmed that 'Society comes into existence that man may live: it continues in order that he may live well,' and that to live well necessarily presupposes glimpsing an end and trying to shape conscious behaviour towards it. Certainly no student of medieval Europe or of the Reformation can doubt that 'ideas' help to form the patterns which history throws up, and that these ideas have legs. Nor can it be denied that there are times when a 'system' is so wrong in principle that its very existence – its way of doing things – is itself prejudicial to the 'end' which it is supposed to serve. All this I take for granted. But at present, that is in the England of the 1960s, theoretical and propositional questions are certainly not the first to be raised when the subject under discussion is the national character of the Church of England.

There is still some significance in the oft-repeated dictum of the historian J. R. Green that the English nation is 'the child of the Church'. The reference, of course, is to the genesis of the nation before the Norman Conquest; to the fact that when the Teutonic tribes came over to England in the fifth and sixth centuries, bringing with them their religion of the Northern forests, they were not long in their new home before the Christian faith was brought to them in the Roman mission of St Augustine. And this mission came with the prestige of the ancient civilization of the Imperial City and at a time when the old gods of the Teutons were no longer adequate to meet the challenging demands or the psychological unsettlement arising from travelling across the seas to an unknown land. The Christian Church sanctified kingship: it suggested that the sanction of law was finally of divine origin; it held aloft a vision of unity while the nation was still divided; it gave witness that the kingdoms of this world live their lives against the background of an eternal order. Moreover, and equally important, the Church provided the only civil service which the State could, for centuries, draw upon; and in the local parish priest, who quite often stepped into the shoes of a pagan predecessor, the central authority had a civilizing and governmental agent on the spot. Little distinction in Anglo-Saxon England was made between the sacred and the secular, between Church and State. The bishop sat in his ecclesiastical court and also in the witan; and he himself could not have told where his 'religious duties' ended and his 'secular responsibilities' began.

Medieval theologians later speculated *ad nauseam* as to the different roles of Church and State, Papacy and Empire: but they did this for practical purposes. So far as the individual citizen was concerned, Church and State were for the most part one and indivisible. No one thought that a man could be inside the one and outside the other. Indeed it is imperative when studying the classic medieval disputations concerning Pope and Emperor to resist the temptation of reading into the words they used concepts and ideas which belong to a subsequent history. Excommunication, in the Middle Ages, cut a man off from society, and removed him from its benefits, in the same way as a papal interdict prevented the full expression of that society's corporate life. Heresy was a serious anti-social crime, and the Church without compunction handed the heretic over to the secular power for condign punishment – which, where there was no repentance, was often death. Dissent in religion, failure to affirm what was accepted authoritatively as a full Christian faith was seen as the introduction of a principle of anarchy cutting to the very heart of the community. Its effect was to undermine the basis on which that society rested: to break its cohesion and weaken its sanction: to prevent it from realizing the God-given end for which it existed. Such an assessment of the need for a uniform Christian profession was not thought to derive from an *a priori* logic, but from reflection upon experience, in particular from a recognition of what the Christian Church had done in generating the civilization of Western Europe. But for this Church, barbarianism might have held sway.

The Reformation, in one sense at least, introduced the principle of dissent or secession: but so strong and deeply embedded was the older concept of the indivisibility of Church and State that the breakaway from Rome was at first contained within homogeneous national churches. The right of the individual person to dissent was nowhere admitted. The religious conflict in England, during the reign of Elizabeth, was not primarily the struggle between rival groups concerned to maintain a separate if minority existence; but over the right to dominate and to lay down the pattern of a national worship to which all must conform. *One Church* was seen as the necessary corollary of an absolute religious truth, and the relationship of this truth to the well-being of men, indeed of society itself, led to the same conclusion. Where the protest against Rome was not so open a breach as it was in Lutheran and Calvinist countries, national rulers endeavoured to deal with the Papacy in their own way – the Spanish kings by imposing a settlement through their possessions in Italy, the French kings through the fiction of a *concordat* and the consequent making of a new one. In England the novel solution was attempted of a reformed, purged, episcopal Church, continuous with its medieval antecedent, but minus the Pope, and with the Sovereign supreme 'over all causes and all persons ecclesiastical as well as civil'.

Yet though so strongly embedded in men's mind, the medieval concept of one Church was not destined to survive in the new Europe of emergent nations. The very secession from the Roman obedience introduced the principle of dissent. Thus the Church of England, given its 'new look' in response to the 'winds of change', and comprehensive though it continued to be, proved unable to contain all the varieties of religious and church loyalty which the Reformation fostered and brought to birth. This was the more so because these differing interpretations of Christian faith had profound political and social implications. Also the Renaissance, the grandest achievement of which was the growth of the scientific method, led to a general weariness with the bloody religious wars which the Reformation sparked off. The result was the birth of a tolerant and secular spirit such as characterized England in the eighteenth century. The liberal state of today was in process of being born.

Yet this modern child took a long time to enter into the mood of an adult security, so conservative is the collective psychology of the group, and so retentive are dominant ideas and customary ways of thought. The unsettling experience to which the nation was submitted, when the episcopal Church collapsed to be followed by a proliferation of religious and political sects under the Commonwealth, persuaded the English people to welcome the less exacting demands of a known system.

Charles II was restored in 1660, and with him the *Ecclesia Anglicana* and its monopolistic privileges. To be a full citizen once again meant to be a member of the national Church.

Yet the logic of events, even if conservative opinion obstinately refused to accept it, was becoming clear. The national Church might remain, but it could not continue as inclusive of all nationals. The reluctant and limited toleration granted to a few dissenters in 1662 was enlarged under the Toleration Act of 1689, which was still meant to be, as its title suggests, a tolerance. It by no means granted full civic rights to those who took advantage of it. What it did was to respect their conscience, but they were required to suffer if they obeyed its scruples. Yet the writing on the wall was plain, though it was not until the nineteenth century that Roman Catholics and Dissenters – and in the end all citizens – had, by statute, their legal disabilities removed, and the Church of England monopoly over the two Universities of Oxford and Cambridge was in the main broken. The Toleration Act of 1689 was, in effect, a realistic recognition that dissent had come to stay – and dissent in this context may be taken as (prophetically) representing a wider dissent embracing all religious professions or none. No longer, even in 1689, was it possible to regard membership of the Church of England as essential to citizenship, though it was still held to be essential to the assertion of a first-class national status. But even the deprivations under the Act of Toleration were in part overcome by such expedients as 'occasional conformity' and annual acts of indemnity.

The effect of all this was to produce a situation unique to the English scene. First it led to the rise of what is called the 'dissenting interest', and the 'nonconformist conscience', both of which have had a considerable and salutary influence upon English social and political life, not the least in bringing to birth, earlier than elsewhere in Europe, what was in effect a pluralistic society. After a long period of quiescence, following the Toleration Act of 1689, the dissenters set out, through political action, to campaign for their own civic rights, and engage themselves as a constant pressure group.

But these dissenters, who came to regard the establishment of the Church of England as their enemy and the great obstacle to their full hopes, were not hot-blooded secular revolutionaries intent upon turning society upside-down. Not even the most fanatical Anglican Tory could honestly see them in this guise. On the contrary, they were serious, sober men, of great moral integrity, who, in the last analysis and where the larger issues of life were concerned, were at one with the 'interests' they opposed. There were differences, of course, between conformist and non-conformist, establishmentarian and dissenter, and these differences were acutely felt: but they were not about final principles, the end which society ought ultimately to pursue, or whether there was any transcendental authority to which men and nations finally owe their allegiance. What these differing interests held in common was more important than what divided them. Both hedged in an absolute authority, vested in the State, with an absolute divine constraint to which men are subject. The phenomenon of a reformed established Church, witnessing to a continuing tradition of total involvement with the State, and at the same time adjusting itself to a liberal and secular society, in which all subjects under the Crown have equal rights, duties and privileges – this is a subtle and complex development which can all too easily be taken for granted. Some assessment of it must affect our judgement as to the place of a national Church in the England of today.

The establishment of the Church of England, and in this context I mean more than its purely legal nexus with the State, even in its contemporary minimal form, did not result from any rational discussion as to the nature of Church and State, or conscious reflection as to their relations with each other. There is no one document which defines what establishment is and what in law it supposes. In fact, establishment now represents the last remains of a system in which a common Christianity was assumed, and from which a vast number of citizens have, at various periods, chosen to withdraw. Indeed, some would see the psychological approach, which is a hangover from establishment, as more important than the precise legal nexus which has gone into the making of it: and would maintain that the former could now continue without the support of the latter.

The fact is that the present situation, for better or for worse, has grown from, and is the legacy of, a long history in which a Church has generated a nation, and the nation has subsequently been submitted to the stresses and strains of living within the political structure of Western Europe. No group of persons, sitting round a table, could have devised, or conceived of, the establishment of the Church of England as we know it. It is significant that establishment, as it now operates, exists within an essentially liberal state, which paradoxically is in many ways religiously neutral; and that, although the status of the Church of England may confer certain privileges, it does not do this by depriving others of their constitutional rights. Maybe the privileges are in fact better understood in terms of responsibilities.

Indeed, an established Church, living alongside non-established (or, as we say) 'free' churches, and among a wider personnel who make no profession of religious faith at all, could not have maintained its status in a liberal society without conceding rights. This has meant that the campaign, led by the dissenters, for a full and complete citizenship independent of any religious profession, did not begin in this country as a doctrinaire assertion of rights, but as the result of the concern of deeply religious men, dealing with a practical, concrete situation, in which by redressing grievances for their fellow-religionists they were able to help others. The course of development here in England was far different from that which has been followed in most other European countries and it has tended to give stability to our political institutions. Government and opposition are not irreconcilables.

Such reflections as the above, however, may at first seem more interesting historically than immediately relevant. But is this so?

Establishment, with the correlative of non-establishment, has certainly contributed to the development of a stable liberal society. But is it in any sense a helpful religious ingredient in the latter half of the twentieth century? This is the question we must now briefly consider.

It may help if we first review the current facts concerning the establishment of the Church of England, and then inquire as to the more subtle psychological attitude which it has brought to birth.

The first of these questions may be dealt with summarily. Establishment in this context means, generally, that the ordered life of the Church of England is built into, and has behind it, the sanction of the law of the land. The Sovereign, who (like the Lord Chancellor) is required to be a member of the established Church, is its 'Supreme Governor' and is crowned by the Archbishop of Canterbury in Westminster Abbey, with the solemn rites of the Church. The clergy of the Church of England, upon taking up their appointments, whether they are parish priests, canons of cathedrals, deans, or bishops, swear allegiance to the Throne, as 'supreme over all causes and persons ecclesiastical as well as civil'.

The government of the Church of England (to repeat what was said above) has behind it the legal authority of 'The King in Parliament,' and thereby retains a national character. *The Book of Common Prayer*, which contains the liturgy, was affixed to the Act of Uniformity of 1662, and it was an Act of Parliament in 1919 which established the Church Assembly, together with the Parochial Church Councils which now exist in every parish.[1] Today any resolution of the Church Assembly which may affect the rights of Her Majesty's subjects, or is thought likely to change the character of the Church of England can be, and certainly would be, debated in Parliament, in the Upper House of which the two archbishops and twenty-four bishops have seats.

Establishment, with its corollary of the Royal Supremacy, also means that nomination to high ecclesiastical office – to all bishoprics and deaneries – rests with the Sovereign, such nominations being recommended to her via the Prime Minister. Other patronage, much of which is in private hands, constitutes a freehold right and as such is protected by common law. The incumbent of a parish acts in part as a civil officer when he performs weddings, and he is entrusted with a pastoral oversight within a defined geographical area. All those who live within it have a right to his services, and spiritual ministrations.

A catalogue of this kind, however, and it is far from complete, may not seem significant or helpful. What it shows is that Crown and Parliament (to put it crudely) have a 'say' in the life of the Church of England and that its organization, and in some respects its worship, have behind them as a sanction the law of the land. If the history, to which I have referred earlier, is ignored or forgotten, such legal facts, interpreted by a pedestrian mind, could easily suggest a Church in bondage; a religious society hamstrung by the shackles of the State; an *ecclesia* under a ruthless erastian domination which prevents it from doing its job or ever discharging a prophetic role; a church holding its title deeds from Parliament.

This view is sometimes taken. But I do not myself see it that way. My own view arises from the conviction that the unique function of any Christian Church is to witness to, and to build, the Kingdom of God through commitment to Jesus. In seeking to do this it must, of necessity, enter into relations with society around it, and directly or indirectly with the State as such.

Even such a strongly separatist Church as the Church of the Mennonites in Pennsylvania find some relationship unavoidable. But the relations into which a Church enters, the *modus vivendi* which it endeavours to establish, the nature of the impac' it makes on the structures of the collective life, will depend on the kind of Church that it is, as well as the state that it lives in, and the nature of their contemporary confrontation.

Such relations will not be determined by logical inference from fixed principles, but by what F. D. Maurice calls 'life and experiment'. This does not mean that we must refuse to ask the question: 'How best can this Church build God's Kingdom in this immediate environment, and what does this seem to imply in its relations *vis-à-vis* the state?' It means that the answer must be sought within the present situation rather than by the injection into it of rigid *a priori* categories from outside.

It is in this kind of pragmatic spirit (though not forgetting that principles are involved) that I, at the moment, approach the question of a national Church, and its legal establishment. There is no normative relation of Church to State, but only better and worse relations within given and particular situations. Excessive formal discussion tends to withdraw either 'entity' from its existential condition. One thing is certain: a Church must be as free as it can make itself to fulfil its primary function. For it to acquiesce through weakness, apathy, or sheer love of ease, in a situation which could be made more favourable to the cause which it exists to serve must always be a grievous sin; and certainly there are occasions when a Church ought to go into the wilderness.

The Church of England is not, by reason of its establishment, in this situation: and I would hazard the opinion that at present the establishment, on balance, enables it the better to attempt its task of building God's Kingdom.

In taking this point of view, I assume that an established status is not wrong in principle, necessarily distorting the whole process of building God's Kingdom. Many relations of Church to State are possible and have existed: it is the Church's responsibility to make certain that the one which obtains is the best that can be contrived, not in some Utopia, but here and now.

Some such modest claim can be made for the national and established Church of England. The present *modus vivendi* is capable of improvement, in the sense that more 'value' relative to the Kingdom might be purchased at the cost of less 'disvalue'. Adjustments can be made, and admittedly ought to be and will be made. But the complete severing of the nexus between the Church of England and the State, in response to a doctrinaire demand for liberty or for the sake of a more tidy logic, could impoverish rather than enrich its witness.

On the other hand, establishment does presuppose a Christianity which is deeply involved in the life of man in society, not simply in the intimacies and friendships of home and family, but in the challenges and ambiguities of man's collective existence. It sees the Kingdom as incarnating itself in the group structures which are thrown up within a modern community in a technological age: it is prepared to face up to the grim fact of power and the harnessing of it to serve the Kingdom. By accepting (or at the lowest not rejecting) a status as national and established, such a Church cannot in the nature of the case see the collective life as irrelevant or impervious to the Gospel of Christ. An established Church cannot even be tempted to regard the Christian ethic as relevant only to man's personal life while leaving his civic and national responsibilities untouched. It cannot – if it is true to itself – affect, for a moment, to despise politics, to see them as essentially a somewhat dirty business; but must hold a 'high view' of them. An established Church recognizes that to serve society governmentally is for some Christians a vocational constraint: and that matters of law within and between States are finally subject to the divine will and need to be lifted into the world of grace. This means that an established Church has at times the responsibility of sitting in judgement and all the time of challenging the State with the claims of God's Kingdom, though it will do this as deeply involved and in no holier than thou spirit.

A time may come when the confrontation of Church and State must of necessity be seen in a different light. The State itself may wish to break the link, because it no longer desires, even in a minimal way, to identify itself with Christian faith; or because, even if it wished such an identification, it no longer desires to do so through an association with one historic Church. Again, a situation might arrive in which a truly prophetic Church that meant business and possessed a real cutting edge could become an embarrassment to a venal State in an affluent age. The Church might find itself hamstrung and in such a situation, disestablishment would become a moral imperative: for the Church must never decline to put itself in a position in which it can effectively work to build God's Kingdom. More simply, to preserve establishment is not and cannot be an end in itself. The *sine qua non* of such a link must be that the State wishes it to continue, and that this continuance is seen by the Church as promoting its primary responsibility of building the Kingdom.

Other chapters in this book will deal with different aspects in the life of a national church. My concern has, in the main, been limited to its historic origins and background, and the particular ethos to which this development has led. Religions, like social patterns, do not remain static, and the move towards a 'reunion' of reformed churches in England is bound to raise again the whole question of the link with the State. It is to be hoped that this discussion will take place within the widest possible terms of reference, of which the social is one.

Nor could a national Church be unaffected by the passing of the sovereign state, and the emergence of some united states of Europe if such should happen. Certainly a Church, with its roots deeply imbedded in catholic Christendom, ought not to find the transition difficult, nor a new *modus vivendi* impossible. But this is a large issue which, maybe, another generation will have to face.

NOTES

1. For the text of the Church Assembly (Powers) Act 1919, (The 'Enabling Act'), The Representatives of the Laity Measure and other Measures on constitutional matters see the Church Assembly Handbook (Church Information Office, 2s. 6d.).

WHY BISHOPS?

1 *Episcopacy*

On the first page of a copy of the Ordinal given to the writer by one of the presenting bishops at his consecration, the bishop had written under his name the words,

'consecrated a Bishop in the Church of God'.[1]

To what and for what is a bishop consecrated in the Church of God? Not to 'bishop-hood', but to the care and oversight of a particular community of persons. It is a pastoral office and he is empowered and authorized to look after that community with the solicitude of the Father whom Jesus Christ reveals. The word 'pastoral' tends to evoke the image of a priest sitting by the bedside of an infirm old lady speaking comforting and cheering words. It is that, of course, but it is much more than that. The care of a community, varied in its composition and life and acknowledging Christ as Lord, even if it is numerically small and localized, includes administration, ordering of worship, jurisdiction, and leadership in proclaiming the Gospel to those who have not heard it or are deaf to it; but it is always essentially pastoral. 'As the Father has sent me, so send I you.' 'You have not chosen me, I have chosen you that you should go and bear fruit.' 'Feed my sheep.' 'Other sheep I have not of this fold, them also must I bring.'[2] So said Jesus; and that is the bishop's commission. The community may elect, but his authority is not from it so much as from him.

By the middle or towards the end of the second century A.D. in the Roman Empire a bishop was the head of the community of Christians in a town or district; and so it continued throughout all Christendom until the Reformation. It was natural and inevitable that the Christian community should copy the order and rule existing in the Roman Empire. By that date the aristocratic republics in ancient Greece and republican Rome were only a memory among the cultured *élite*. The bishop of a church was its father-in-God, sustaining its members in a time of persecution, and leading its missionary enterprise. He was also its ruler. He had colleagues and counsellors, but the last word was with him. He governed by virtue of his *episkopé*, which was his spiritual inheritance from the Apostles; and not by virtue of his election or appointment.

While almost unconsciously this form of government followed the pattern of government in the state, consciously the second-century Christians looked back to the Church of the Apostolic Age and to the choosing and commissioning of the Apostles by the Lord Christ Himself.

Some students of the N.T. think that the writers of the Gospels, and the contemporary Church at the end of the first century read back into our Lord's day the pattern of order and rule which was already beginning to take shape. This is an unnecessary hypothesis, for it would be natural and needful that Jesus should select from the larger group of followers a small group of men with a latent quality of leadership, and that as the shadow of the Cross began to fall across his path he should hold them close to himself so that both by living with him day by day, listening to his conversation and teaching and learning his way of thinking, they should grow into his likeness. This is what St Paul meant by 'having the mind of Christ'. They had a great deal to unlearn about authority and kingship and to learn about the royalty of service before they could receive and understand. Before the Crucifixion they had not fully understood these things. The strange horror of a crucified Messiah shocked them as Jews to the core of their being so that for a moment their loyalty faltered and they fled. The Risen Christ, by the power and mercy of God, restored their confidence – a hundredfold.

Apart from the N.T., we know little about the growth of the early Church from the time of St Paul until a clear pattern emerges a hundred years later. This was partly because the

Christian communities were fragmented under severe persecution and were only held together by apostles and itinerant preachers and by faith in their deathless Lord. There is also little in the N.T. about church order. The reasons for this silence on a subject on which the ecclesiastical mind is voluble is chiefly that the early Christians were persuaded that they were living at the end of history, and not, as it has proved to be, at the beginning of a new era, which already has gone forward for as long a time as the O.T. goes back. Believing that in a very short time – within the lifetime of most of them – the Lord would return in glory to usher in the new era, they did not bother much about 'establishment' and order. They concentrated on more important matters, which are still priorities, faith in Jesus Christ and the life of the Kingdom for which they had to prepare. By the end of the second century, however, this belief had become a hope deferred *sine die*, and meantime questions of order and the need for authority such as a monarchical episcopate provided were becoming urgent. One reason for this was the strength of gnosticism which was a deflection from Christian faith, plausible and with the seeds of death in it. By that date it was a firm belief that bishops were the successors of the Apostles and that this authority was sanctified and assured by the consecration of every new bishop through the prayers and laying-on of hands of several bishops including the bishop of the chief church in the region who came to be regarded as the metropolitan.[3]

The process and the speed by which this position was reached varied from place to place, and the mists lie thickly over this period of history. As the N.T. is also indecisive in its evidence, theologians and historians could continue to disagree in their interpretations until the end of time If the need for exact knowledge about the development of Church Order is as important for the Christian mission in the world as theologians in their disputations have thought it to be, why, one wonders, did Providence allow it to be wrapped in such obscurity?

Leaving this vexed question and moving towards our own

times, it is important to note as Gregory Dix has pointed out that the *constitutional authority* of the bishop has remained more or less the same down the centuries but the character of *his administrative authority*, i.e. the way he does his job, has naturally changed a lot. The constitutional authority of Bishop Lightfoot of Durham last century was similar to that of St Cuthbert 1200 years before, but in administration very different. Lightfoot, scholarly, administratively wise and far-sighted, directing and going to and from Auckland Castle; Cuthbert, going about with his band of monks, converting the heathen, confirming and instructing the faithful; at the end dying in his cell among the birds of the Farne islands a little apart but loved and revered by his monks who lived across the water at Lindisfarne and within hearing of the distant bell that announced his departing.[4]

There are many ways in which the bishop of a diocese may faithfully carry out the duties of his office. How any one man does it will depend on his personality and gifts and also upon the character of his diocese and the circumstances of his time. I am persuaded that a diocese should be of a size to allow a bishop of normal capabilities to know and be known by all the clergy of his diocese; to know their differing jobs and to be known in their parishes; a father-in-God not in name but in fact, so that there is a mutuality of affection and trust, freedom in discussion and cooperation in planning. In order that he may really know the clergy of his diocese and what is going forward in the parishes as a co-pastor, which is what he is; and in order that he may exercise his *episkopé* in the total life of the community within the geographical bounds of his diocese he must both care a great deal and also stay a long time so that he feels identified with its life and the people feel that of him.

In the early Church a bishop stayed in his diocese till he died of old age, unless he was convicted of heresy or was martyred. In the Roman Church that is still the expectation – from the Pope downwards. This is not a law written into the structure of the Church, but a deeply-rooted custom – even a *mystique* of a sort of marital relation 'for better for worse, till death us do part'. 'Till death us do part' raises practical difficulties, especially when the relationship becomes 'for worse' rather than 'for better'. Nevertheless a bishop is not just a dignitary, or a district superintendent, he is the father-in-God of a local Church or See[5]. But the doctrine only becomes meaningful – and how much discussion about apostolical succession fails to be! – when episcopacy is not merely talked about, but practised in such a way that the members of a diocesan family learn to care for one another and think and act together, and the family spirit deepens and ripens because its succession of bishops have been truly fathers-in-God after the apostolic pattern.

If that is not the case I cannot see that there is a worthwhile argument for keeping the Church divided over episcopacy. Why should we think that the Holy Spirit after 1900 years of monarchical episcopacy should not be able to invest the functions and authority of *episcopé* in a corporate body like a presbytery? That, indeed, would be nearer to the authentic spirit and doctrine of the apostolic ministry than reducing the episcopacy in a united church to a congerie of district organizers or treating it as a sort of civil service.

Since Roman and medieval times men have learned the techniques and manners of group discussions, friendly dialogue and conciliar decisions, especially in countries where for generations there has been a free democracy. This compared with customary behaviour both in Church and State up to a short time ago, is a new temper and mode of common action on which men have come to rely. The Society of Friends has shown the authoritarian churches how to effect unity in action by waiting upon the Spirit. In the Church all this is an initiative or experience of the Spirit which should influence discussions on authority and order; and lead to a closer working partnership between bishops, clergy and laity in a diocese together with a diocesan and cathedral staff, sometimes formally in Synod, and more often informally.

In the considerable discussion in church circles at the

present time about 'synodical government' the essential point is the one made in the previous paragraphs – that bishop and clergy, and as far as possible laity of both sexes should be a friendly working partnership in a diocese. This is achieved as a rule more successfully and at deeper level by informal than by formal methods.

The reason why the British Constitution has worked so well for two hundred years is because of the imponderable elements and informal opportunities for conversation and consultation which are not written into the Constitution or the standing orders of Parliament. This is particularly evident in the House of Lords where the procedure is very little by rules and standing orders but chiefly follows a tradition of common sense which is remarkably flexible. This also applies to local government and until the Church Assembly came along it applied to the Church of England. This informality is a distinctive element in the political genius of the English people – and very precious. It explains why those who have tried to copy the British Constitution on paper as it were have found that it does not work when transplanted as well as they had hoped. Lord Hugh Cecil and his colleagues unfortunately overlooked this when they tried to model the procedures of the Church Assembly on that of Parliament. None the less the Church of England seems to get along more democratically these days than Churches which are more synodical and formal in their procedures – and in consequence tend to be less flexible and more easily dominated by officialdom.

While synods are a good thing to have from time to time as occasions demand (and more informal conventions of all the clergy and workers of a diocese even more) there are reasons for doubting whether 'synodical government' will quickly achieve what some hope it will.

1. It will be necessary first to reduce large dioceses (by the formation of new ones) to a size that will allow a synod of *all* the clergy in a diocese to be small enough to allow real open discussion and to disallow mob oratory. And even then it is not easy to make an issue so precise in a resolution that either

'yes' or 'no' is a fair answer. If this is not successfully done then time can be wasted by a string of small amendments. Moreover, in these days a synod must include the laity. If lay representation is not limited to the lay clerisy – which God forbid in a national Church – it is not easy to see how the laity can be truly representative without a synod becoming a *kirchentag* of unwieldy dimensions. Some diocesans, there may always be who start dull and end by being tiresome and others who start with democratic intentions and end by being autocratic. But when the worst has been said of us and allowed, let it never be forgotten that the diocesan bishop in our English inheritance is the safeguard against a centralized bureaucracy and oligarchy, and a protection from the dictatorship of a *curia* from which the Vatican Council is trying to release the Roman Church.

One other thing: democracy is in danger of talking itself to a standstill and being smothered in typescript. In universities and colleges; in the medical services and one suspects in industry, men and women are being drawn away from the work they have been trained to *do* and ought to be doing, to talk and listen at committees, to sit on councils and conferences and to read voluminous mimeographed reports (which would be only half as long if those who produce them wrote them out first instead of dictating them). In the Church of England today an unconscionable amount of time is being taken up with this sort of thing and diocesan bishops are the chief victims. The Church Assembly proliferates councils and committees. It needs to practise birth-control. The weakness spreads to the dioceses. 'Something must be done', it is said, and instead of following a good precedent and responding, 'Whom shall we send', or 'who will go', a committee is appointed.

Ten or so years ago the writer occupied himself on a sleepless night counting up the number of nights he had slept away from home and outside his diocese, other than on holidays and specific speaking engagements. He was horrified to find that it added up to about sixty days and nights. On looking back on these meetings and the journeys to London, York, etc. they entailed, he thinks much of it was wasted time and might have been better spent on quiet reflection, and getting about the diocese and seeing more of its clergy and laity and making more contacts across the Christian frontier. So he is allergic to the thought of adding synods to the list, even while he is wholly in agreement with the aim of getting together and thinking together.

While a bishop is primarily the bishop of a specific See, his responsibilities are not confined within its boundaries any more than they should be restricted within them to the clergy and their congregations. A diocese is a complete unit of the Church – bishop, clergy and laity – but no more self-contained and exclusive than any Christian family should be. A bishop is consecrated into the service of the whole Church of God. As far back as the third century the provincial system began to develop. The diocesan became one of a college of bishops with a collective responsibility especially in matters of liturgy and doctrine. The bishop of the chief church in the region became metropolitan – *primus inter pares*. By the time of the famous Council of Nicaea in 325, a consecration was not valid unless it at least had his approval. Thus Constantinople and Rome came to have the pre-eminence. Gregory Dix makes a comment upon this development, not without warning for us today, 'the new system promoted administrators rather than leaders. And there can be little doubt that it was the new irresponsibility of bishops towards their flocks which made possible the interminable distraction of the Church from her missionary task.'[6]

In the Church of England the diocesan bishop has a responsibility towards the whole Church and this is well understood. Today there are in addition the demands made of a bishop by the ecumenical movement not only within his diocese and within the country, but also beyond national frontiers. This widening range of responsibility will affect his thinking and prayers as well as influencing his engagements and taking him out of his diocese. This is as it should be; but nevertheless he will lose touch with the laity of his diocese, and still more with the community in which it is set, if he is absent from it too often and for too long. And loss of touch of course means loss of influence. It is a matter of striking a balance and of delegating and sharing responsibility – and how that balance is struck will partly depend on the gifts and interests of each bishop. But today only partly: for the incipient bureaucracy at the centre, and the Church Assembly that has brought it into being, are making demands on the time of diocesans which are unreasonably excessive and plainly wrong, not only because they ask more than most men can compass, but because they put pressure on a bishop to get his priorities wrong. It is not desirable that diocesan bishops should be expected always to be chairmen of the increasing number of boards, councils, commissions and committees, because, or partly because, being members of the Assembly they can report to it on behalf of the bodies of which they are chairmen. The services of many competent laymen might be used at the national level. And it would be for the C.A. to allow such chairmen who are not members of the Assembly and have not time to be, to address it on behalf of their boards or councils as required. Similarly within a diocese. When the writer went to Sheffield in 1939, the bishop had been chairman of every board or committee of the diocese, and there were only two or three laymen of much standing in the community upon them. Not much could be done about that in wartime but when the war was over he made over some of the more important chairmanships to laymen. In his experience laymen in top positions are very ready to help the Church if they are given responsibility and not just asked to be yes-men on a committee which is presided over by a bishop and on which the majority of its members are clergy.

Finally an English diocesan bishop has a responsibility in and towards national life which is only partly discharged by occupying a seat in the House of Lords when he gets there and occasionally rising from it when he has something pertinent to say in a debate – though that is not unimportant. If each of the bishops in the House kept himself well-informed on some aspect of national and international life in which he was genuinely interested and so could speak on it with conviction, as Cyril Garbett used to do on housing, and not just to a brief prepared for him it would be greatly appreciated in the House, and his voice would carry beyond it – speaking to a brief prepared for him is very second best.

My own conviction is that there is a strong case for holding to our episcopal inheritance in the Church of England as it now is, provided the House of Laity in the Church Assembly and the Crown lawyers allow us to make the best of it and not just the worst of it, and provided the Episcopate does some fresh thinking about itself.

A functional condition for doing this is not to spend money in building up offices in London with increasing staffs or just to multiply bishops until they are six a penny in the land, but to increase the number of dioceses; and at the same time to insist that adjacent dioceses begin to share some of their administrative and financial services, and do not feel compelled to sink a lot of money on building new cathedrals or expensive episcopal residences.

The Church of England – maybe other Churches are the same – still has a persisting capacity for spending its money on obsolete impedimenta with the result that it never has enough money for the new ventures and initiatives that a time of rapid change and a new era demand. It is the dustiness of that kind of 'establishment' mentality that we want to blow out of our windows in the English Church and in the English mentality; not the basic nature of the Church–State relationship that we have inherited. For it is to the radical changes being demanded by the needs of the world today and to-morrow that churchmen should be giving their minds, and to the quality of bold, sustained leadership that the Christian mission requires in order under God to come to fruition.

All the denominations, indeed, are too occupied with the supply of fuel for the domestic hearth and new furnishings for the house; and in the Church of England our attitudes are unconsciously affected by the continuous repetition of the obsolete social concepts in the Prayer Book. Another debilitating influence in the past upon episcopacy has been that of the lawyers whose duty it was to be jealous for the Royal Prerogative. Not so long ago, a group of bishops who had spent many hours on commissions and committees concerning training for the ministry had become convinced that a man with the status and experience of a diocesan bishop should be appointed to give all his time to this work as chairman of that department. The choice and training of ordinands is a chief responsibility of the Episcopate, but in recent times it has become a much more complex business financially and in other ways. Forty-two bishops trying to do it corporately would with the best will in the world waste a good deal of time and energy falling over one anothers' feet. Better that one of their number who was obviously qualified, should be allowed to resign his See in order to do this on behalf of them all. We were given to understand, however, that to resign a Crown appointment to fill such an office might appear to be disrespectful to the Crown and seem to be exchanging a pastoral office for an administrative one. Some churchmen might fear that such a proposal if it became a precedent would lead us up the path which has led to Roman Curia and the practice of the Roman Church of using bishops in specialized posts. But the Roman Church is careful to maintain the principle of the pastoral nature of the episcopal office by allocating to every bishop – even to those who have retired – a titular See. And in the Anglican Communion in the U.S.A. the bishop chosen to be 'Presiding Bishop' resigns from his diocese. The thin end of the wedge argument is a fallacy induced more often by fear than by reason.

The case for preserving our episcopal inheritance would also be strengthened if clergy and laity would release diocesan bishops from the more trivial engagements which they thrust upon them. Bishops know only too well that a multiplicity of these use up time and strength which should be given to the reflection that a long-term planning and sustained leadership require – and to unhurried dialogue with one another as befits a collegium, and also with men and women exercising in other walks of life influence in the nation.

As things are diocesan bishops are under great pressure to substitute short term tactics and little bits of salesmanship for a thought-out strategy of engagement with society as it is and is likely to be tomorrow. In my time I have taken part, I should guess, in more than a hundred meetings of diocesan bishops, formal and informal. It is a happy memory of friendly association in which differing opinions could be discussed with good humour and fair debate. Some of the subjects discussed were of urgent passing importance; others of recurring importance. But I cannot recall many occasions when we really faced the revolution in English society since the Book of Common Prayer was promulged in 1662, or the radical change in thought and belief and in the pattern of life since the industrial and scientific revolutions; and in the light of these changes, the need for a new policy of engagement and penetration. Linked with this demand to lead the Church in a missionary initiative there is also the responsibility to encourage the new thinking that science is requiring of theologians and the changes in the liturgy of the Church that must ensue.

A national Church and its leaders have a special responsibility; for they still have unique opportunities and points of personal contact at the parish, diocesan and national level with the life of the people.

2 How are the Diocesan Bishops Appointed and Consecrated?

As many people have vague ideas about the procedure of appointment and some have erroneous ideas it might be well to describe precisely, and yet without too much of mere protocol, how diocesan bishops in the Church of England arrive at their posts. The simplest way to do this is to detail the course of events in the one case which the writer knows at first hand, for the procedure was the normal one at that time, excepting for the outbreak of the war.

The previous Bishop of Sheffield's resignation took effect in July 1939 when he was in his 82nd year. On 15 June I received a letter from the Prime Minister, as follows:

Dear Archdeacon Hunter,

The See of Sheffield will shortly become vacant by the resignation of Dr Burrows and it is my duty to submit to His Majesty the name of a successor. After the most careful consideration, I have come to the conclusion that I cannot better serve the interests of the Church than by offering to you the succession of this important See. On hearing from you that you will be willing to accept this offer, I shall be happy to submit your name to the King.

Until His Majesty's approval has been obtained, I have to ask that you will treat this matter as confidential.

Yours sincerely,
NEVILLE CHAMBERLAIN

I had not met the P.M. before the letter came, and never saw him afterwards, and I had no enthusiasm for his statesmanship at that time. Two days later, letters came from both Archbishops. Temple knew me intimately as we had been in contact ever since I 'devilled' for him in the office of 'The Challenge' twenty or so years before, when he was its editor. The letter is characteristic of the friendly letters Temple often wrote in his own hand – so here it is:

My dear Leslie,

I have just heard of the letter that has been sent to you from Downing St. I want you to know that it was with my most cordial approval that this choice was made, and I very much hope you may see your way to accept it. The only ground of hesitation which I can imagine weighing with you seriously is the difficulty in which the diocese of Newcastle may be placed. I think I have some understanding of that, but I am quite sure that it ought not vitally to affect your decision.

I will not say more about that now, but wanted to say so much so that you should know that this aspect of the question had been in my mind.

Yours affectionately,

WILLIAM EB OR

The Primate of All England wrote at greater length and with more protocol – 'This offer is made with my full knowledge and concurrence' – and said a good deal about Sheffield, which had been in his diocese during his early years at York. He also knew me and had been most kind when nine years before I resigned my parish owing to a long illness.

The eighteenth was a Sunday, and on the days following the Church Assembly was meeting. I went up on the Monday and stayed with 'Jumbo' Parsons, the Bishop of Southwark; and it was arranged that I should see Archbishop Lang the following day. In his study at Lambeth he talked to me as a true father-in-God. Before he dismissed me, he made me kneel down beside his prayer-desk, and prayed very simply for me and for both dioceses, and gave me his blessing.

Of course, I saw Temple, and I also talked with a lay friend, and wrote to B. K. Cunningham, the wise man of our Church in those days, whom I always consulted when decisions had to be made.

The Archbishops knocked down all my arguments for staying happily where I was and produced some strong ones for going to Sheffield – so did the others. In due course, I wrote to the P.M., accepting his offer, and received a further one from him to say that he had written to the Sovereign. By the same post came one from his secretary to say that the appointment would be announced on the following Saturday, and suggesting that we might meet and make one another's acquaintance, and discuss 'the conditions prevailing in Northumberland'.

So much for an appointment that was a fair sample of the way in which diocesan bishops were appointed twenty-five years ago, and of the association of Church and State in the choice – which is even closer now. It so happened that the only one of the persons concerned with it on the side of the State whom I had met was King George, for I was one of his chaplains, and had had the experience, unforgettable for me, but probably not remembered by him, of spending the New Year week-end with the Royal Family at Sandringham eighteen months before.

Why do priests accept bishoprics, one is sometimes asked. If a man has become a priest because he could do no other and believes that only the Christian faith can save the world from itself, one may accept what is considered a wider sphere of Christian service, especially when those whose judgement he trusts think that he should; while another may refuse, either because he is sure that he ought not to leave what he is doing or because he has special gifts and interests which would in measure be set aside in a diocesan bishopric. In my own case I did not want to move. We had become deeply attached to Northumberland and its people and were absorbed in the problems of industrial Tyneside. I enjoyed the worship of Newcastle Cathedral and liked being Archdeacon of Northumberland, an office that goes back to the twelfth century and linked one with the ancient See of Durham. South Yorkshire on the other hand was *terra incognita*. But forty-nine was a good time of life to make a big change if so advised. Undeniably a diocesan bishopric does provide responsibilities in church and society which may under God become opportunities. It is also a truth about life, in the words of André Gide, *'que le bonheur de l'homme n'est pas dans la liberté mais dans l'acceptance d'un devoir.'** So, without too much about vocation, that was why.

The Cathedral Chapter of Sheffield had, in due course, to go through the motions of receiving the King's *congé d'élire* and solemnly electing the man of his choice as their 'bishop and pastor'. This Tudor hang-over most people regard today

* Preface to *Vol de nuit* by Antoine de Saint-Exupéry, is a summary of the theme of that book.

as meaningless and rather blasphemous and think that it ought to have been annulled years ago.

Thereafter, there was correspondence with the Archbishop of York about the date of the Consecration, and whom he should invite to do this and that, and with the authorities of York Minster who were kind enough to allow me some say in the choice of music and hymns. We stayed with the Archbishop and Mrs Temple on the night before, and the previous afternoon I had to endure the very legal ceremony of 'confirming the election' after which the bishop-designate legally has a right to exercise some of the bishop's administrative powers. The Crown Appointments Commission in its report recommended that this ceremony should be modified and that the date of his Consecration should be legally the date when he is invested with the rights, duties, etc. of his office.

In my own case the outbreak of the war threw a dark cloud over the Consecration. To kneel before Archbishop Temple and to have his hands and those of bishops who were to be my colleagues placed upon my head; to be surrounded by friends – clergy and laity from Northumberland whom I was leaving at that grim moment in history, and by clergy and laity from Sheffield who were to become my care – and in that sublime church to wait upon God in the beautifully ordered Eucharistic offering of worship, was a deeply moving and inspiring moment in my life. Enthronement in Sheffield Cathedral took place on 14 October, and ten days later at Buckingham Palace, I was presented to His Majesty by the Home Secretary according to custom, and did homage – Geoffrey Fisher at the same time having done homage on his translation from Chester to the See of London – and a few days later I received a beautifully inscribed missive declaring that the temporalities of the See were now mine.

It is with reluctance that this bit of autobiography has been introduced as it sounds egotistical. If, however, the writer's episcopal contemporaries were to dig into their files they would unearth a story and correspondence so similar as to make the difference in time and circumstance and persons of relative unimportance. Moreover when so much that is less than half-the-truth is said about the subject it is important to run the risk of being misjudged and to be factual.

To be contemporary, there is this to add: since 1939, a systematic practice of sounding diocesan opinion has been established by the Prime Minister's appointment secretaries. When I obtained, in October 1961, Her Majesty's leave to resign on the following 31 March, I was asked to give verbally and on paper factual information about the diocese and to arrange for the secretary to meet with people in the diocese. At the end of November he spent two days with us, during which he met the full Chapter of the Cathedral and also had individual and private talks with seven of the clergy and eight of the most responsible laity in the diocese – these latter happened to include the Lord Lieutenant, who was Chairman of the Board of Finance, the Vice Chancellor of the University, the Chairman of the N.E. Coal Board, three other leading industrialists, and the chairman of the Magistrates. He also met the Lord Mayor, who was a senior Trade Unionist, and outside the diocese he saw two clergymen who had spent many years in the diocese and had recently become dignitaries in other dioceses. No doubt the information the Secretary acquired was put at the disposal of the Archbishop. The thoroughness of the consultation and the way in which it was done made a most favourable impression. The greater the surprise and disappointment when three and a half months elapsed before an appointment was offered, accepted and announced.

In the appointing of bishops selection is more important than election, and Consecration far more important than either. There is, none the less, a strong though imprecise feeling in the Church that it would be more democratic and more spiritual if bishops were elected within the Church. In many parts of the Anglican Communion there is no alternative to some form of election. In the Scandinavian countries where the Crown appoints there has in recent times been a procedure for nominating from a Church body three names to the Crown: and a reverse procedure whereby the Crown submits three names to a Church body has also been canvassed. Their experience shows that the limitation of nomination or choice to three names does not get rid of the disadvantages of election. The disadvantage is not only that it provokes partisanship and then as a way out of an impasse it often leads to colourless appointments – its hurtfulness lies in the whole business of electioneering, especially where it has 'news' value in the press.

Church history shows that ecclesiatical human nature is exposed to some weaknesses and passions to which ordinary human nature is not so prone just because it is ordinary. Electioneering can be nasty and hurtful in ordinary life: in the Church it can become spiritually hurtful and evil. Moreover, if by 'democratic' is meant 'one man one vote', then it is not all that easy to decide the qualifications of the one man, least of all in a Church which is in some relation to a nation. Then if it is felt that a large electorate for the nomination or choice of a father-in-God is not desirable, the alternative of a larger body appointing a smaller body of electors, and perhaps that smaller body choosing a quite small body is not a democratic procedure, but has proved in history to lead to oligarchy. Be that as it may, men whose judgement is informed both in the Scandinavian Churches and also in many provinces of our own Communion think that the Church of England is indeed fortunate to be spared the distresses of appointments by election, and that we would be wise to accept our fortune as long as a good understanding between Church and State continues, and the Church has a decisive, though not necessarily a deciding, voice in selection. It must also not be forgotten that in the last resort the Church has a veto if the archbishops (and bishops) were to refuse to consecrate. If the Church is thoroughly, competently, and, prayerfully involved in the selection of priests for the higher offices then it is not irreverent or unspiritual to trust to the operation of the Holy Spirit especially in the case of the consecration of bishops.

Concerning selection there is something more to be said. One of the important functions of a diocesan bishop is to know his clergy and to have a care for their growth and development. There are some men who will only fit small jobs, and they are not to be discounted for neither church, state nor industry could function without them. Experience of public life, however, shows how often men grow in stature when more responsibility and a wider sphere of activity are given to them at the right time. We are discovering that all too late in the life of the country, as educational opportunity is now becoming open to every young person capable of responding to it.

In times past many priests of potential gifts were left too long in restricted parochial jobs. It is for the well-being and vigour of the Church's impact on society that there should not be this wastage. While the best preparation for a job with wider responsibilities is to do the job one is in as well as one can, it is, for example, good that a parish priest, without being tempted to neglect his parish should be encouraged to widen and deepen his range of interests and experience, and be encouraged to do so. The life of the whole Church would be enriched and strengthened if clergy were more often engaged with the life of the world on a wider front and at a deeper level and knew more about what other Churches are doing in this and other lands. But this is a little aside from the point that part of a bishop's function is to know his clergy, to help them to develop and to recognize those that might fill more responsible posts not only in the diocese but beyond it.

If selection for the higher posts is to be as good as it should be the time has come when all this needs to be done, diocese by diocese, more systematically. The bishop's list of 'possibles' for higher office should not only be of his own making, but should be made in consultation with knowledgeable clergy and laity in his diocese, and be reviewed annually. Such lists from all the dioceses would be open to the whole episcopate and would provide the central list from which men for appointments might be selected. This should be the corporate responsibility of the episcopal collegium, even though the final nomination may go through the Archbishops or a particular bishop, and a layman may have the responsibility of keeping the list fresh and in order. The existence of such a list and procedure would never prevent an individual churchman making a recommendation direct to the Prime Minister's secretary.

The subject of Crown Appointments was thoroughly explored during 1962 to 1964 by an Archbishops' Commission on which the writer had the privilege to serve. Within the existing framework of the Church – State relationship the Commission proposed the abolition of relics of Tudor usage and some reforms both of statutes and also in procedure which would give the Church more say in the filling of these posts and might thereby strengthen its whole ministry. It also considered carefully alternative proposals and procedures in other Churches.[7] After debate at several sessions the Church Assembly decided on the recommendation of its Standing Committee in November 1965 to defer decisions on changes in regard to Crown Appointments that would require legislation until they could be considered in the wider contexts of the whole Church – State relationship, and the place of the Royal Prerogative in it, and of the movement towards church reunion. It resolved to ask the Archbishops to appoint a commission 'to make recommendations as to the modifications in the constitutional relationships between Church and State which are desirable and practicable and in so doing to take account of current and future steps to promote greater unity between the Churches'.

Desirable reforms in the manner of appointing, however, will make little difference if there are not sufficient of the right kind of men to appoint and if those who decide what is the right kind have the temper and approach which is often eminently safe rather than inspired, and if they are thinking of an England that no longer exists. The useless slaughter of so many young men in the 1914–18 war might not have happened if leadership had not been conditioned by a strategy and tactics that had become obsolete. The Church of England is in a similar predicament.

The breakthrough will come, not if we put our trust too much on appointment secretaries, but when the collegium of archbishops and bishops are so fully seized of the new situation confronting the Church that they refuse to ordain men to the ministry who lack the spirituality and outlook of an apostolic ministry.

3 Bishops Who are not in Charge of a Diocese

In the early centuries there were no retired bishops – the best got martyred before they reached old age. There were no assistant or suffragan bishops – 'a bishop', said St Cyprian (martyred in A.D. 235) 'is constituted by his church and a church by its bishop.' There were no translations from See to See.[8] The first known instance of a translation is that of Alexander of Cappadocia to Jerusalem, and it was felt to be so exceptional that it had to be justified by a miraculous vision. When the practice began to be more frequent in the fourth century it was denounced by a series of Councils (including Nicaea) and was disapproved by the purists as a sin akin to adultery. For historical reasons translations from one See to another are more frequent in the Church of England than in other episcopal churches or in other parts of the Anglican Communion. In the Church in the U.S.A. translations are not allowed – and it is to be hoped that they will hold to this rule which has a weight of tradition and pastoral experience behind it.

In the Roman and Orthodox Churches in the past diocesan bishops have rarely retired, both for reasons already mentioned, and also for the practical reason that there was no pension available. The latter reason also operated in the Church of England. Until 1926 the only pension which a bishop or incumbent might get was at the expense of his successor. With the permission of the Crown, a bishop on resigning his See might claim up to a third of the income, which was hard on the See especially if it happened to be encumbered with a palace. So retirement was a rare occurrence, and there was no problem either for bishop or church as to the service the one might give to the other.

The usual practice of the Roman Church has been to keep a bishop as father-in-God of a diocese till the end of his life, providing a younger episcopal colleague to take over most of the executive duties when the senior one became old or infirm. This colleague might be a coadjutor with the right of succession, or an assistant who might move. It is a practice in some respects comparable to what happens in large commercial and industrial undertakings where a managing director or chief executive officer moves into the chairmanship of the company and perhaps eventually becomes its honorary president.

This practice of retaining local expertise and pastoral contacts may be better and more Christian sense than the proliferation of suffragan bishops, which at the moment seems to be the Anglican choice. The Church of England, and indeed our country, has clung too long to a belief in the value of amateurism. It looks outmoded and is handicapping in a technological age. The Church also clings quite absurdly to an eighteenth-century belief in discontinuity. Months are allowed to elapse between the date of an incumbent's or bishop's resignation (or death) and the successor's institution or enthronement. Consequently valuable personal contacts are lost, and impetus slows down to a standstill. These changes are affected more rapidly in the Roman Church partly because its ministry is celibate. Archbishop Heenan, for example, passed recently from Liverpool to Westminster within a week. In the comparable services of the Navy, Army and Air Forces, such dilatoriness would not be tolerated. Perhaps the argument for coadjutor bishops is that not only does it enable a man to learn the techniques of the charge of a diocese before he has its sole charge, it also preserves valuable personal contacts between church and society, and a reasonable continuity in policy. Let it be said bluntly that the Church of England in a missionary situation cannot afford to continue to be as complacently haphazard and administratively incompetent in the use of its resources as it used to be.

The institution of a proper pensions scheme whereby bishops become eligible for pension at seventy – and it is being suggested that the age might become sixty-five – is going to confront the Church of England with a new situation to which as yet it has not had the inclination to give thought. Men are living longer than they used to do and are beginning to retire earlier. In a few years there will be twenty or thirty bishops who have retired from the charge of a diocese at an age when they should have ten years before them during which their wisdom drawn from a long and varied ministry, their spirituality of it has not been drained away by activism, and their mental powers if exercised might continue to be of service to a Church impoverished in man-power. How best this should be done requires thought and experiment, but it should not prove a difficult exercise.

There are positions in life – the judiciary for example – where wisdom, patience and knowledge are more valuable than the ability to act promptly and rapidly. The Roman Church not only retains its bishops in their dioceses, it has always relied on a few elderly men at the top to guide and direct, or to use for special assignments. The average age of its cardinals is over seventy. Many popes have lived beyond that age and a few like the late Pope John have shown after eighty remarkable vigour and ability to get things done.

By contrast in the Scandinavian Churches, bishops and clergy become pensionable like civil servants and the tendency is to think of them as such. Hitherto the Establishment here has thought similarly. The day a bishop resigns his See he drops out like the civil servant and the only link he has with the Establishment is the quarterly cheque for his pension. A top-ranking civil servant can take another kind of appointment, and indeed his experience and service are in demand. A bishop, however, is not a civil servant and he remains a bishop and pastor to the end.

The Church of England will have to develop a policy and

practice of using some of its bishops between sixty-five and eighty, more flexibly and intelligently according to their interests and gifts. They might, for example, be used in the Anglican Communion and ecumenically for *ad hoc* assignments, and as consultants and advisers. In the years ahead there is need to supplement official assemblies and discussions on faith and order by more unofficial and informal penetrations across political and ecclesiastical boundaries. They might be used to relieve diocesans of some of the excessive amount of committee work that is being thrust upon them. Two or three, if they had the attitude and interest and if the State would allow, might retain their seats in the House of Lords provided they agreed to attend regularly when the House is sitting, for as things are diocesans simply cannot do this. They might share their ministerial experience with ordinands and clergy, and even with bishops-designate and newly consecrated. Finally, there is the need at all levels and at all ages for the ministry of the Church to be fully engaged with the world and to step beyond the Christian frontier. Most diocesans are conscious that they have not been able to use the many opportunities which they have of doing this – the failure is not always due to the wrong choice of priorities, but to sheer pressure of work. Here is another continuing ministry of an informal kind which a man with episcopal standing might be encouraged by the Church to pursue. On an earlier page (80) it was suggested that there might be one or two full-time posts of responsibility which a diocesan bishop might be asked to fill before he reaches the normal age for retirement and which he might continue to hold for some years after.

If in these ways and in others, the Church began to use its older men more intelligently, after they withdraw from full-time posts, notably its diocesans, then a recognition of this would be to divide a bishop's pension as it is into 'pension' and expenses of his continuing service in the Church. Be that as it may, the Church in its engagement with the world will have to deploy its resources in man-power with a better sense of strategy and with more imagination in the new age than it has done hitherto.

NOTES

1. Bishop R. G. Parsons, at that time Bishop of Southwark. He had also added to the inscription in the book, 'Feast of St Michael and All Angels, 1939. Isa. xl, 31. John xx, 21'.

2. John xx, 21; xxv. 16; xxi, 17; x, 16.

3. The literature is immense. Within our own Church:

H. M. Gwatkin, *Early Church History*, to 313.

K. E. Kirk, (edited by) *The Apostolic Ministry*, especially the long section by Dom Gregory Dix on '*The Ministry in the Early Church*'.

Fr A. G. Hebert (written shortly before his death) *Apostle and Bishop*, Faber and Faber, 1963.

Stephen Neill, *Anglicanism*, Penguin Special, 1958.

4. Lightfoot, *Leaders of the Northern Church*, pp. 73–86. Sermon on St Cuthbert spoken in 1885.

5. A bishop's see is the ecclesiastic unit committed to his charge – his diocese or seat of office. In the Roman Church every bishop has a See, but sometimes as in the case of a retired bishop it may only be titular.

6. *The Apostolic Ministry*, chapter on the Ministry of the Early Church, p. 279.

7. *Crown Appointments and the Church*, Church Information Board, 1964, 7s. 6d.

8. Quoted by Dix in the chapter mentioned in note 6.

THE CHURCH IN THE
LOCAL SITUATION

1 *Towards a New Reality*

THIS chapter sets out to show that it is possible and right to build on the fact that the Church of England *is* established, and that on these often merely vestigial remains a new series of links at the local level of society as it is and as it is becoming may be created. If this can be done we shall at least have a modern phenomenon rather than an ancient survival to consider, and a position full of potential advantages to both Church and community.

In the past the idea of the established Church meant that there should be at every level of society from the monarchy to local parish a built-in, though often fairly informal, link between the secular and the ecclesiastical. In the rural areas a benevolent and paternalistic rule could be, and was, exercised by squire and parson. This rule could extend to a censorship of morals and to other areas of life in a way which we should find unthinkable today. On the other hand, bad feeling between the Hall and the Rectory could produce misery and failure of such system as there was.[1] In the towns there was a strong connexion between the secular government and the Church of England. Many vicars served on the bench and as chaplain to the mayor or corporation. Innumerable welfare schemes, small charities, almshouses, and doles for the poor were administered by the mayor and vicar acting together. Church rates were both a practical reality and a symbol of the establishment of the Church. Financial links are often the most cogent proof of other connexions, and it is worth noting that a local authority could and did contribute to the building or re-building of a church.[2]

This is not the place to describe in detail the gradual decay of the idea of the established Church locally during the nineteenth and early twentieth centuries. The three great eroding forces were the educational controversies, the development of social welfare legislation and the growth of the Labour and Trade Union movements towards positions of power in local affairs.

In each of these features of social life one may distinguish two elements – first, the recognition of the sheer size of the problem which is gradually seen to be beyond the reach of voluntary effort, however devoted, and second, the accompanying growth of secular autonomy in the various fields of doing good and caring adequately for all members of the community alike. Thus, in the field of education, the necessity of providing schools for all the nation's children reduced progressively the Church of England's share in the honourable effort towards this end. This fact of the size of the problem, coupled with the unhappy controversy over Nonconformist rights, meant that the Church of England could never again exert so much direct power in the educational system. On the other hand, however, we are left with the considerable potentialities of the 1944 Act with its recognition (reinforced, for example, by the more recent Newsom Report) that the Christian Faith and Christian worship should have a central place in the teaching of our children.

It is an ironical fact that in the field of social welfare also the extension of the fundamentally Christian insights of equal rights and care for all men according to their needs should have been accompanied by a decline in the influence of the Church of England during the past century. Here again this decline was due to the size of the problem coupled with the notion of the secular authority as having absolute duties in this field. The great out-pouring of social welfare effort by church people in the second half of the nineteenth century was still not sufficient for the vast and growing needs of the industrial cities.[3] The idea of social legislation based on state responsibility gradually took its place alongside the idea of personal or church responsibility for ministering to the needs of society. The Liberal Government of 1906 and the Labour

Government of 1945 leap to mind as the most active in the field of social legislation, and the Welfare State, a slow, gradual and continuous creation, came into being most particularly because of the activity of these two governments. Old Age Pensions, National Insurance, the beginnings of a medical service, care for the welfare of school children and many other social services date from the work of the Liberal Ministry of 1906 and onwards, and thanks to the pioneer thinking of Lord Beveridge, the Welfare State as we know it developed from the legislation of 1948. So there was brought into being a whole army of social workers, who rightly pride themselves on their high professional standards, and who undertake the care of those in need to an extent never before achieved and far in advance of anything that the churches can now attempt. They are in fact the natural successors of the Christian pioneers of the nineteenth century.

The legislation just referred to could be implemented only because during the nineteenth century a workable system of local government was rather tardily created out of a complex series of school boards, water boards and the like. The County Councils Act of 1888 and the further creation of Urban and Rural District Councils in 1894 (following the pattern of the Municipal Corporations Act of 1835) provide an administrative basis for an increasing range of local government powers and permissions – responsibility for such services as public health and sanitation, housing, libraries, art galleries and museums, and finally (1902) for education. A new statutory authority was gradually created, a power which so far the Church of England has never really successfully engaged at the local level in the way it had been involved with earlier social structures. It is this power with which the Church must be deeply concerned today.

At the same time, there was growing up a new and powerful force in local government which knew and did not care for the previous deployment of power, especially in the field of social welfare. The Labour and Trades Union movement (which now controls over half the local government agencies

of this country) felt that it had reason to be suspicious of the
Church of England, because of its known relationship with the
Conservative Party. They also felt far from grateful at even
its well-meant attempts at social care.

It is worth while trying to understand the underlying causes
of this attitude, for if we can do so we may be able to overcome
some of the prejudices on both sides in this problem. The
basic attitude of the Church had been paternalistic and
'charitable' in the narrow sense. Many of the best efforts of
Christian social work had been concerned with ambulance
provisions. It is probably a fair statement of the emerging
views of the Labour movement that they saw social justice
as one of the rights of man, not as dependent on (a problem-
atical) charitable effort. They also felt (rightly, apart from one
or two exceptions) that the Church of England would not face
the question of the reorganization of society but would
continue to tinker with relief work in a fundamentally unjust
social order.[4] So the Church, and especially the Church of
England, was hampered even by its charities, and the most
usual cry of the Labour representative up to the 1950s (still
occasionally heard today) was 'If we need anything, we'll pay
for it ourselves' (i.e. out of the rates and taxes). Many voluntary agencies, especially those which had grown up in the
nineteenth century, found themselves under a cloud. It became
clear to all concerned with the social life of the nation that
neither the churches nor any other voluntary agencies could
any longer cope with the basic social needs of a whole nation,
and other means had to be adopted. The onus of proof that a
voluntary service was necessary was therefore now on the
volunteers themselves. Many good church people were
naturally hurt and puzzled by the developments taking place,
and there was for a time a risk of mutual suspicion and anti-
pathy between the new welfare agencies and the old, often
Church or Church-inspired, agencies.[5]

It seems indeed to some church people that from the point
of view of both the worship of God and the care of the
neighbour the sense and reality of the national Church has

gone. True, there may still be an annual civic service in the parish church, the mayor may appoint a clergyman to be his chaplain, and the council business may start with prayers. True, the various Education Acts give authorities the power to co-opt a representative of the Church of England to the Education Committee (though with a fine impartiality the same treatment is given for the C. of E. as for the Roman Catholic and Free Churches). But by and large the present-day local sense of the Church–State relationship has to be discovered and worked for in new forms.

The situation is, in fact, full of promise because, as I have indicated, the fundamental Christian insight of care for the neighbour is now established deeply and by Act of Parliament in the life of our nation, and the situation is wide open for fresh understanding between Church and civic authorities in the local community. If the Church in its organizational aspect were to opt out the loss would be tremendous to both sides. There would be the danger of a loss of the compassion and care that now marks the life of our local government representatives and officials; and for the Church the loss would be even more severe – the loss of a sense of responsibility for the society in which it is set at its most significant point of need. What then can Christian laymen and laywomen do?

The basis for the discovery of the nature of this new relationship at the present day is the involvement of Christian lay-people in the actual work of local government and in the other points of influence in the community. In other words, what was previously built into the actual fabric now has to be achieved through the normal processes of modern democracy and social organization. This may seem to be something of a truism, but unfortunately it is still a novel idea to a large number of church people, and several misconceptions have to be cleared up in their minds before much progress can be made.

The first and fundamental idea that has to be conveyed is that Christians must enter local government and other forms of community service on a level with and not on some fancied terms of superiority to their non-Christian or non-practising colleagues. They do so because (like most of their colleagues, irrespective of belief or religious practice) they wish to serve their neighbour. It would be fatal if they were to try to form a Christian, or worse still, an ecclesiastical 'lobby' or power bloc. (In this way our view tends to be different from that held by many Roman Catholics.) Christians do not take into public life either a monopoly of truth about public affairs or a prescriptive right to harangue their colleagues about their Christian beliefs. They must be loyal party-members (if they are not, their influence will be very small), and must work as efficiently as their colleagues in the day-to-day chores of committee work if they are to help the Church once more to a position truly 'established' in modern Britain.

What difference, then, does being a Christian make in public life? One of the best things on this topic came from a woman City Councillor who said, 'The only thing being a Christian does for me in my work as a Councillor is to make me less elated by success and less depressed by failure.' This is a true Christian insight, but in addition there is undoubtedly for those who involve themselves in local government and other forms of public service the conviction that here is a realistic way of caring for one's neighbour, and that only as the members of the Church are servants of modern Britain[6] can there be a true basis for the Church to be 'established' in it.

What of the relationship of the official Church (which at this point in time still means the clergy) with the public representatives and paid officials of the borough, county or district concerned? It is important that the clergy should see this as a relationship of many strands, most of which they have to make for themselves.

First, there is the necessity for friendship and, in its broadest sense, pastoral care, so that the New Testament command that we should pray for all in authority may be carried out with understanding. Local government representatives and officers carry a heavy load of responsibility, and it is important that the clergy should have a sympathetic understanding of the problems involved. Conversation with public men about their work will give the clergy an insight into some of these problems, and though one may sometimes see a tendency to exaggeration and self-dramatization there is also no doubt that many people in local government deeply value the opportunity to talk freely about their position. When one considers that men in public life are responsible for large expenditure and far-reaching schemes and that they are targets for attacks by their own party, the opposition, the ratepayers and sectional interests, it becomes very important that there should be sympathy and understanding on the part of the clergy. A clergyman who is a good listener can be very helpful.

In addition to the pastoral care of those in authority, there is the Church's duty to promote thought, discussion and in due course practical suggestions about local problems. Here it is important that the attitude of the Church representatives should be one of willingness to learn – and this not only from the public representatives but also from the paid officials. In these days a good deal of time is needed if we are to understand the workings of the statutory provisions of the welfare state, and the vital part which the Church has to play in the whole set-up. If a clergyman gets to know the officers working in his town or parish, from the Chief Officer to the local visitor or field worker, he will soon find areas of life where cooperation is not only desirable but essential to the working of both Church and secular government. In particular, the welfare and education services will be the obvious fields of cooperation, and whereas the statutory social worker has all the power of legislation and financial support, the clergyman has the great advantage of seeing whole personalities in their home and family setting in the parish. He can therefore help the movement already under way in the field of social work from the 'sectional' type of work where a social worker is not allowed to deal with problems outside his area of human need, towards the consideration of whole families and their need within whole communities. (The most recent Children Act presses this movement forward.) There will in fact be little progress towards a new establishment unless the clergy know and have learned to cooperate with health visitors, maternity and child welfare workers, hospital almoners, education welfare officers and teachers, children's officers, civic welfare and other old people's welfare services, housing managers and their staffs, mental welfare officers and the probation service. The list sounds, and is, formidable. But these are the new pastors of our people, and unless we know and are known as having an integral place in this array we must not be surprised if many of our parishioners think of us as marginal to society and its 'real' needs.

Much can be done to establish mutual understanding and respect. Informal meetings between the clergy and social workers will at least introduce to each other workers who are entering the same houses in a parish. Once a happy working relationship is established there can be a good deal of cross-reference of families and people in need, and the work of caring for people made more successful. And indeed the needs are great. The pioneer work done by Miss Helen Roberts, for example, in Birmingham and now in Sheffield has shown that the statutory and other established social workers very much need help if their work is to be done to best advantage.[7] In the course of the Birmingham survey it was discovered in the sample area studied that one family in four was in need of some kind of friendly help over and above that which was being provided by the existing agencies. Here is a great field for Christian ancillary effort to make the welfare state provisions more effective. And more recently Miss Roberts's work in Sheffield in setting up a 'Good Neighbour' scheme has revealed the same need for Church voluntary work. This scheme, covering an area in Sheffield of about 100,000 people, was organized when about one hundred lay-people of different communions (including the Roman Catholic) offered their services to the social work agencies as good neighbours in any case of need. In the first year of working about 130 cases were referred by social workers to the volunteers. The volunteers have proved especially useful in visiting chronic cases, sitting in with elderly people in order to give a younger relative some time off, and helping at week-ends when many of the social services are out of action. This cooperation of church people has been much valued by the social workers concerned, and marks one way in which the traditional partnership between church and community may be re-established.

What should be the attitude of the Church of England today to professional social work initiated and carried on by ecclesiastical organization? For example, should every effort be made to continue the work organized by the Church of England Council for Social Work, still often referred to as 'Moral Welfare', or should this work be handed over as soon as efficiently possible to the local Medical Officer of Health? It is possible to give different answers to this question. If the work is done well it can provide an authoritative standard of excellence in the field of the social services, and also give a standing-ground to the Church for relationships and dialogue with other social work agencies. (A parallel case in the educational field is the Church's decision to maintain and expand the church training colleges.) On the other hand, the general pattern of progress in this country has been for the Church or some other voluntary agency to institute work which is seen to be useful and is then taken over by the secular authority. But whichever decision it is seen to be right to take about a given agency at a given moment, it is of great importance that the Church should always be a working partner in the field of social welfare; and this means that fresh experiments should be made and new initiatives taken in this field.

At the present time, for instance, the statutory services are being slowly overwhelmed by the size of the problem of mental welfare, and both general practitioners and psychiatrists agree that it is not possible to give adequate treatment and after-care to large numbers of mentally sick people. Here the voluntary services of help and friendship offered by the Telephone Samaritan service (Anglican in inspiration) is playing a part in many areas in helping society to cope with its many mentally and emotionally disturbed members, and many volunteers have learned a new relationship with the statutory bodies and a new sense of relationship between Church and community.

So far nothing has been said of the Christian social worker. He or she occupies a key role in the modern version of the Establishment at local level and it is for the Church to recognize this role and to help the social worker to live it out. (Only too often in the past those Christians engaged in social work have gone on with that work without much understanding from the Church of which they are members.) One thinks, for example, of the Family Service Unit movement, Christian pacifist in its original inspiration, which has deeply influenced the whole field of social work, by its method of long-term untiring friendship for problem families, friendship clarified by psychiatric and other forms of modern case-work knowledge. Such pioneer initiative should be supported in every possible way by the Church.

At present many social workers are feeling and expressing a great need for a re-thinking of the basic assumptions of their work. The reasons for this are plain. Most of them come into the work because of a Christian vocation to serve God and their fellow-men. In the course of their training they are quite rightly exposed to modern thought in the realms of psychiatry and sociology. They are then plunged into the world of case-work in which many problems and difficult personal decisions face them. It is most important that the Church in its organized aspect should understand the area of the debate about the nature of man, human personality, and about the role of the social worker in the organization of the modern world, and take a constructive part in those debates.

The Church has survived because, among other excellences, it out-thought the world in which it was set. Again, our task is to institute thinking – to provide the means whereby social workers, doctors, town-planners, teachers, indeed all the new 'clerisy' of the modern state, can think out their basic assumptions, and look at their leading problems. Every time the Church of England, acting through one of its members, clerical or lay, takes the initiative in promoting thought about one of these areas of life, a step towards a new Church–State relationship has been made on the basis of the old standing-ground.

There are of course many other areas of life where links have to be made if our claim to be an established church is to have any reality. One must think of the great 'principalities and powers' which over-arch the merely local situation: the Trade Union Movement nationalized industries such as coal and railways, the great public corporations and limited companies which influence or dispose of a great proportion of the labour force of this country, down to the local firm whose policy or prosperity may have a great effect for good or ill on the life of a parish.

In dealing with all these it is important neither to be daunted by size nor to believe that detail does not matter. Before we can preach or even talk to the modern world it is necessary to understand how it works and how its people think. Much of our preaching and communication today is ineffective simply because we do not understand the people to whom we speak, nor the world in which we all live. Thundering prophetic periods and even authoritative declarations out of Holy Writ fall on deaf ears simply because they have no relevance. But the reward that comes when we try to live in the world as it is today, and when we have understood some at least of its detail, is that we can speak in friendship and with sympathy to the people who are running it. Sometimes we can reveal to them the fact that they are not far from the Kingdom of God. Like Monsieur Jourdain in *Le Bourgeois Gentilhomme*, who had been speaking prose all his life without knowing, some of these people have been living by Christian doctrines without knowing. Sometimes, when we have made the right relationships and know our facts, we can speak a prophetic word against some evil or defect. Most often, we can encourage people to think afresh, in the light of their experience, and of the Christian understanding we can give them, how they can live out their lives in the pattern of the Gospel, which in the last analysis means more efficiently for the service of the world today.

2 *An Editorial Note on the Rural Parish*

The parish has been the geographical unit of communal life and of the Church's ministry throughout Europe for a thousand years. As it is originally a rural pattern, something must be appended to the foregoing chapter about Church and community in the country. The outline of the pattern is most clear and its appropriateness self-evident where the village or township with the 'out-bye' farms has been a self-supporting and self-contained unit with the parish church as the focus of its religious life and its incumbent an integral part of and penetrating influence in the whole life of the community. Here was the establishment *par excellence*.

Chaucer in the *Canterbury Tales* drew a portrait of a country priest which is true for all time; and it would be wholesome if every country priest had it stored at the back of his mind and brought it out from time to time as an exercise in self-examination. It concludes, some readers may remember, with the lines,

> He waited after no pompe and reverence,
> Ne maked him a spicèd conscience
> But Christe's loore and his Apostles twelve,
> He taught, but first he folwed it hym selve.

In those rough days, the parish priest may have been dependent on the lord of the manor for his exiguous livelihood and was often rudely handled by him when bishop or abbot did not defend him; but the fact that he shrived rich and poor alike gave him a spiritual authority that none cared to dispute, even when his ministry fell far short of Chaucer's standard.

The presence of men more or less after that example in the parishes of Europe century after century has been immeasurably more important an influence than issues over which ecclesiastics and politicians have argued and fought. This has been true of men so widely different as 'a stickit minister' in the Presbyterian Kirk of Scotland or a fiercely puritan, self-denying saint of God like the Curé d'Ars in France a century ago.

The parish system and ministry survived the controversies of the Reformation in all countries. When it was fully restored in England after the interlude of the Commonwealth by the Act of Uniformity and its persecuting penalties, the unity of the rural parish was of law and more rarely of grace. The spiritual life of the common people was sustained, at first secretly out of sight and then above ground, in Independent and Presbyterian chapels, Meetings of Friends, and subsequently by Methodism. Nearer our own time the organization that the Wesleys gave to their movement gave Methodism a stability and cohesion. Where 'Independent' congregations of their several kinds have often fallen by the wayside the Methodist chapels have endured. It has been the good fortune of England that its one revolution was not an anti-Christian uprising and that in the following centuries when the established churches were closely linked with *l'ancien régime* and dominated by the men of property there was a vigorous and spiritual non-conformity. And more than that: the legends on the seventeenth and eighteenth century monuments in an old country church often commemorate godly men and women with a sense of social responsibility according to their lights, comparable with the sea-captains of Captain Fox's time who, so to say, kept a Bible in one pocket and a Prayer Book in another, and knew how to read both in 'hours of peril on the sea'. The Squire–Parson axis, and the authoritarian rule of incumbent, church-wardens and the manor-house often was a benevolent and beneficient paternalism; and it did not prevent a pride in and devotion to the parish church even on the part of those who did not conform. The gradual disappearance of the Squire–Parson partnership, and the disengagement of parish priest and church from a paternal feudalism, coming as they did before the twentieth-century transformation of rural England, have been a great gain – one might even say a reprieve – to the established Church. Today the country vicar's axis-partner is, if he interprets his heritage truly, the village community and his sphere of operation not only the vicarage and church but its whole life.

None the less the established Church in the country has had to contend with two major problems during the last hundred years. The first was domestic. From 1870 onwards the number of born-and-bred countrymen entering its ministry has grievously diminished as the state of some vicarage gardens is witness. Consequently many country parishes have had to be staffed by townsmen. Some of these never understood or entered into the life of the rural community. Some offended the conservatism of the countrymen by changing the style of worship in the church. In such cases, their freehold and the fact that they were not dependant on the parishoners for their income underlined their isolation. Causes such as these made the pastoral ministry ineffective and its influence small with the result that the size of rural congregations diminished at a time when the chapels were also in trouble. The urbanization of the country in recent years may have lessened this domestic difficulty, but it is bringing others, as well as new opportunities.

The village and rural parish are no longer self-contained communities. The normal drift of young people to the town has been intensified by motor transport and the mechanization of agriculture. Ploughman has become mechanic, and horses are disappearing from the fields. In most villages, probably in all villages within fifteen miles of a sizeable town, men and women working on the land or with livestock have become a minority of the population. An increasing number travel long distances to work in the town. The senior children are now being transported to schools not in their own village.

The commuter traffic is not just one way. Those who work in towns in ever larger numbers are taking to the country and take with them an urban mentality – though the fact that they are drawn countrywards may be a significant reaction from urbanization. Deeper in the country, many of the agricultural workers' homes have become week-enders' cottages. Added to all this there is the congestion and upheaval caused by the motorist at week-ends and by tourist traffic in certain parts of the country. Quiet, static village life rooted in the soil is almost a thing of the past. If this stirring has brought gains it has also brought losses, which the Church must try to lessen.

The country in more ways than one has fed and nourished urban society. Therefore the efforts made during this century to stimulate country life and make it more interesting for young and old by the building of village halls, young farmers' clubs, womens' institutes, rural community councils, various cultural activities, have been very worth-while.

When vicar and churchmen take the initiative that the establishment allows, together with the schoolmaster or mistress if there is one, they can give to the village community a unity and a stability combined with a liveliness of temper and an interest in life beyond its boundaries. It requires that the priest should not be a bird of passage but should be deeply integrated in the communal life. It does not matter if his sermons are repetitive so long as his prayers are real and his concern and care for people keep warm and fresh.

Fortunately the antagonism of church and chapel, which was as much political as religious, is dying out, and it is for the local establishment in the spirit of Christ the Servant, to take the initiative and to see that it does. In the old days the nave of the village church was used, and the church bells rung, for a variety of occasions, secular as well as religious. If the problem of times of service could be amicably solved, and the law could be reformed, there is no reason why the walls of the parish church might not echo the hearty singing of the nonconformists of the community as well as the more decorous sounds emitted by conformity. Even now the village church is still 'our church' to the villagers, conformist and nonconformist, where they assemble on community festivals, and which they subscribe to repair when the passage of time makes that necessary. The Hebrew prophets and the great seers of the Church like St Francis were both conformist and non-conformist towards the faith and the tradition – not without deep tensions. So should a national church always be.

In a changing village, incumbent and parish church can in the best sense be a stabilizing influence well-rooted in the earth and nature, as well as forgiving and redemptive. When one sees areas of rural France where, partly as a result of dis-establishment, some villages have no resident priests and in the old churches the Mass is rarely said and offered, one realizes that in spite of mis-uses and sins against charity, the Estab-lishment with its endowments in this country has been a blessing; and might, if better used in this time of transition, be even more so. But the Church must not too lightly substitute a motor-cycle for a vicarage. It must draw more countrymen into its ministry and train more ordinands specifically and intelligently to serve a life-time in the country, content to enjoy some of the amenities of urbanization with the help of TV, and inhabiting a well-designed, labour-saving house where the villagers are welcomed.

In 1961, agricultural workers in the United Kingdom numbered 664,900; the population in rural areas was less than 10 per cent of the whole; agriculture contributed only 4 per cent to the gross national product. To those who measure a country's wealth only in terms of yardsticks and dollars rural areas and many village communities will be reckoned to be no longer viable. Livestock should be removed from the fields, and tied up in factories to produce more meat for urban bellies; the depressions of arable land, the valleys, and the rivers should become catchment areas and reservoirs; the villages that are not well-sited for commuters or for industrial development should be pulled down and just a few kept as homes for retired folk, or as places of interest for tourists to visit like some of the old country-houses, the Roman Wall and its camp-sites. The Church of England instead of station-ing 51 per cent of its clergy in rural areas should reduce the numbers to the 10 per cent or whatever the proportion of the whole the rural population is.

If, however, there are values in life which cannot be measured by yardsticks and in dollars, including some material things like food-production on an island, then some urbanized economists, sociologists and bureaucrats will have to think again and more historically and profoundly.

There are in truth values in the total life of a society which it cannot lose without ceasing to be human and civilized. Reverence for life – animal life as well as human – livestock as well as wild animals; the enrichment which comes when families strike their roots deep into good, clean earth; the understanding and appreciation of nature; the quality and texture that life acquires when it is lived in a smallish community at a not-too-rapid tempo; the intrinsic value of good craftsmanship, whether of the farmer's wife baking bread, or of skilled manual crafts; these and their like are worth, both to individual and community, more than their weight in gold. They are 'beyond money and price' and cannot be reckoned in the coinage that counts up to 'a gross national product'.

Appreciation of nature and earthiness like 'faith, hope and charity' are values that have to be preserved in order to achieve 'a genuinely human solution of the problems of society'. This valuation of life is far removed from being romantic about green fields, nostalgic about the good old days, or unscientific. It is hard fact and true realism.[8]

In order to strike a fair balance between urbanization and country life in an industrial age the nation needs some men and women who will bring love of nature, reverence for life, appreciation of some cultural values which a rapidly urbanized society is in danger of forgetting and losing, to the study and solution of rural problems. This is a vocation and responsibility for the Church. If some of those being trained for service in the country were also trained in the expertise of economics and sociology (and horticulture) they might stimulate intelligent thinking and practice in rural areas. By helping to preserve values in civilized living near to the heart and mind of Christianity, they would be serving both town and country well.

NOTES

1. Crabbe's tales give us a realistic picture of the early nineteenth-century version of the Establishment at work or breaking down on personal or religious issues. See especially 'Advice; or the Squire and the Priest'.

2. Doncaster Borough Council contributed about twenty-five per cent to the cost of re-building Doncaster Parish Church after the fire in 1853. In our own days, Coventry Cathedral received nothing from the local Council, but Lincoln Cathedral has recently received £1,000 from the Grimsby Borough Council.

3. See, for example, *Evangelicals in Action*, by Dr K. Heasman.

4. See *The Ragged Trousered Philanthropists*, by Robert Tressall.

5. One did not know whether to laugh or cry when an elderly town parson said in 1949: 'My people used to come to me to borrow bed-pans. Now they get them from the Welfare State.'

6. Mention has been made of local government. This is intended as one, perhaps the best, example of public service today. Naturally the work of magistrates, hospital councils and voluntary welfare organizations are more appropriate fields of activity for some.

7. See *Responsibility in the Welfare State?*, Birmingham Council of Churches.

8. cf *The Land*, by V. Sackville West.

THE ECONOMY OF THE
CHURCH OF ENGLAND AND
ITS MINISTRY[1]

A GOOD deal of attention is being given inside the Church of England, and beyond, to a study entitled *Deployment and Payment of the Clergy*[2] which, published in 1964, is the thorough work of Mr Leslie Paul, a writer with a good head and a lively pen, who loves his Church and who, in his younger days, was the *fons originis* of the title, an angry young man. With the passage of years Mr Paul's anger has become tempered by charity; his radicalism and reforming zeal, though unabated, are better documented. The title of the book, moreover, was hardly of his choosing. The Church Assembly asked that the Central Advisory Council for the Ministry should 'consider, in the light of changing circumstances, the system of the payment and deployment of the clergy,' and to make recommendations. The Council, which might be expected to have the expertise to do this, thought more modestly of its own abilities and employed Mr Paul to do it for them, leaving him free to do it in his own way. The Report is also interesting to those who are not primarily concerned with the Church of England's domestic mis-managements in that the writer looks at the economy of the Church in the context of the contemporary climate of thought and of the changing social pattern, and, being a good Christian, not without reference to moral principle.

It does not detract from the value of this study or its timeliness, that the facts – broadly speaking – which it brings to light are not newly discovered and the main recommendations which they justify have been argued among us since before the last war. Indeed it is those among Mr Paul's sixty-two recommendations which are novel that are most debatable. In 1937 an anonymous, but not uninfluential group of churchmen published *Men, Money, and the Ministry* – a plea for economic reform in the Church of England.[3] It produced lively debate in the dioceses and led to further publications, notably *Putting Our House in Order* (1941). These two publications received the general assent of Archbishop Temple and twenty-six bishops, and of many well-known clergy and laity.[3]

Partly in consequence of this 'campaign' Archbishop Lang at the request of the bishops appointed in 1941 a commission, which was reappointed the following year by the House of Bishops, 'to advise that House on certain matters relating to the legislative and administrative machinery of the Church of England'. It was specially invited 'to examine the most practical ways of securing (1) fairer remuneration for the clergy of all ranks, (2) some limitations of the freehold of the clergy, and matters relevant to either, or both of these objects'. It was a strong commission of eleven persons under the chairmanship of Bishop Bell of Chichester, and included Archbishop Temple, until he was translated to Canterbury, Bishop Haigh of Winchester, and two other diocesans, two of the Church's financial pundits in Archdeacons Bradfield (subsequently Bishop of Bath and Wells), and Cyril Twitchett, the First Estates Commissioner (Sir P. Baker-Wilbraham), and the Secretary of the Ecclesiastical Commission (Mr, now Sir, John Brown), and the Principal of St Edmunds Hall, Oxon, Lt-Comdr Emden.

It worked as quickly and thoroughly as Mr Paul has done, and had the files of the Ecclesiastical Commissioners at its call. This Report[4] raised and studied closely most of the issues that are discussed in the Paul Report, and its recommendations were also far-reaching and not dissimilar.

The Commission is convinced that those are in the right who believe that one primary condition of progress, in dealing with the pay and remuneration of the clergy, would be the acceptance of the idea of pooling – diocese by diocese – benefice endowment and capital trust funds for the maintenance of the ministry, the income from which should, in the interests of the Church of England as a whole, no longer be retained by certain benefices.[78]

It recommended:

(1) That the Christian duty of giving for Church purposes, and particularly for the support of the ministry, should be taught systematically to every member of the Church.

(2) That wherever possible annual grants from central and diocesan funds should be made conditional on local contributions.

(3) That a bishop should have power to refuse institution to any benefice for which he and the diocesan authority consider that an adequate income cannot be guaranteed.

(4) That in every diocese each parish should be invited to contribute voluntarily some percentage of its receipts either towards the stipend of its own incumbent or towards the stipends of the ministry generally.

The Commission, with the help of the staff of Queen Anne's Bounty[5], went very thoroughly into the problem of the unsuitability of many parsonage houses, and asked that Q.A.B. should

use any available money in or towards alleviation of post-war dilapidation charges, in cooperation so far as possible with the parishes concerned; and that the Ecclesiastical Commissioners or Q.A.B. or both of them should tackle the problem of 'improvements' on new lines, with new standards of accommodation and construction, and the greatest possible elasticity of administration; and for this purpose to set aside a substantial capital sum over a period of (say) twenty years.

It also proposed that in each diocese a small expert committee should without delay make a precise inquiry what moneys could be found and contributed to raise minimum stipends and do the other things required. Its final conclusion was that

if all available resources are used to meet the present need; if parishioners can be made to feel the urgency and are thus awakened to a new spirit of giving; and if the problem of the parsonage house is tackled resolutely, with the help of an adequate capital fund: then we believe that it should be possible to lift the burden of financial anxiety which now weighs so heavily on so many of the clergy.

The members of the Commission were sure that the lifting of this burden would release spiritual power and would give the Church an elasticity in its economy which would better enable it to fulfil its function in the new pattern of society that would emerge in the post-war world.

It was remarkable that a Commission which contained some men who were not reformist by temper and principle should have been so unanimous. One of the early achievements of William Temple after he became Archbishop of Canterbury was to get this Report generally approved by the unanimous vote of the House of Bishops. It was probably only the untimely death of Temple which prevented a radical programme of reform being agreed upon immediately after the war, and receiving the spiritual and moral impetus to carry it into operation. Instead eighteen years have been lost. Some of the changes that were advocated have indeed been effected; the Church being driven by sheer economic necessity. But the changes have come too slowly, and have not been as closely related either to the mission of the Church in society or to rapid social change as, quite rightly, the Paul Report thinks they should be.

My fear is that the reforms urged in that Report which are more than ever needed may again be held up if the debate is conducted in terms of ways and means and administrative improvements, not to mention appeals to the self-interest of individuals and groups. What set some of us alight in the 'Men, Money, and the Ministry' campaign before and after the outbreak of the war were two simple and basic principles inherent in the Christian faith. The economy of a Church should, as far as human frailty and the temporal circumstances allow, reflect and express the Christian pattern of corporate life and should enable it to use its resources in such a way as to make the national Church an effective Christian influence in society. Industrial friends have always been very indulgent towards one's advances as a bishop. But, however tactfully one might make suggestions about the set-up of industry, one was wide open to the riposte, 'But, look at your own show,

Bishop!' – especially if we were talking not just of functional efficiency but of moral principle. Or to put the point more piously, reforms in the Church involving money, bricks and mortar, terms of employment, social relations, at bottom concern the holiness of the Church and its witness to Jesus Christ in the world.

The other truth which should inform discussions and decisions about the economy of the Church is this. The Church is an ancient institution which like all ancient institutions has a *natural* tendency to inertia. Therefore a resolute dealing with the properties, revenues, and the general establishment of the Church would be a corporate expression of its faith and obedience to Christ as no pietism can be. It will release spiritual power as no amount of hortatory eloquence can do. For the Spirit of God always breaks into the life of individuals and committees at the point of action – when without fear or favour or delay they do what they know is right. 'This do, and thou shalt live.'

What then according to Paul, or not according to Paul, should the Church of England, without fear or favour, or delay, do in regard to its manpower and ministry?

1. *The pooling of the various funds available for the payment of the ministry, and the devising of a rational scale of remuneration from the newly ordained deacon up to deans, bishops, and archbishops.* It is not beyond the wit of Christian men to work this out so that it makes a clear and intelligible pattern and at the same time has sufficient elasticity to fit varying situations and circumstances. This would have the additional merit of ironing out the oversharp distinction between beneficed clergy with a freehold and unbeneficed clergy without one. It would also strengthen *esprit de corps.* When this change from endowing benefices to using endowments to remunerate men was first put forward there were cries of 'bureaucracy' and 'a civil service.' But it really was nonsense. A scale of payments which is generally accepted as fair and applies to everyone is no more bureaucratic than unsystematic, variable and irregular payments resulting from historical accidents. One difficulty in

the past in making a change of this kind has been that the larger part of the Church Commissioners' income was money held in trust for this or that benefice. In the last twenty years, however, the income of the Commissioners which is untied has been much increased, and diocesan and central funds are now augmenting the stipends of most of the parochial clergy. In other words a pooling which seemed a drastic change twenty-five years ago is already more than half accomplished, so that it will not be a big operation to complete the process, and should be relatively painless.

2. *Re-deployment of clergy.* Once the pooling of income has been achieved then the Church can consider realistically the deployment of its clergy. The tables of statistics in the Paul Report show how little this is related to density of population. The staffing of rural areas of course must show a better ratio of parson to population if the Church is to function effectively in them. Is the difference excessive when there is a shortage of clergy? The figures suggest that it is. In 1961, the ratio of parochial clergy to population was 1 per 3,249; in a rural diocese it rose to 1 per 1,120, while in some thickly populated areas it fell to 1 per 6,000+.

Even less defensible is the unbalance within urban areas. Thirty-three years ago, the parish of Barking had a population of 51,000 and in the previous year we were trying to serve it with a staff consisting of an incumbent with three curates and two women workers. At the same date the population of Exeter was similar and it was being served by nineteen incumbents and a cathedral staff. The pooling of the income from all sources will not remove these differences (often in remuneration as well as in man-power) but it will make a re-deployment more possible.

Statistics also make clear that the greater the density of population, the poorer the results by any and every yardstick. This is not the only cause of the alienation, or at least the absence, of the artisan and the unskilled worker from the corporate life of the Church of England, but it is certainly one cause. In many an industrial area where forty years ago a parish was worked by an incumbent with two or three un-married curates, now there is only an incumbent trying to serve a population of 10,000, 15,000, and even 20,000, and the worshipping congregation less than 1 per cent of a popul-ation and hard put to keep its buildings warm and lighted and in repair. Moreover as a result both of new housing and the demands of industry, the population has become very mobile. Some of this mobility may lessen as people settle down in new housing areas and new estates, but the movement from the old and central districts of urban areas out to newer housing areas will be continuous. Thus the Church finds itself with many old, or oldish, churches in urban parishes from which the population has gone, and many of the benefices are well endowed, while in the housing areas it lacks buildings and endowments and man-power. The contrast is also marked between the staffing of parishes in affluent districts and sub-urbs and those where the manual workers live, and the new and populous estates where, in the beginning, especially, a large staff is desirable. The building of large blocks of flats creates yet another problem. In an artisan area the people in them may in time develop a social life, but in richer areas each household tends to keep to itself.

3. *The parish system is not obsolete but it is not sufficient.* Ideally the ecclesiastical parish, and *mutatis mutandis* the diocese should be a social unit. In the old days, especially in rural areas, it often was also an economic unit, with its squire and parson and pub, and later on its school and its chapel. In the towns also, and not only in the small market town, the parish was often a social unit. But modern industry and transport have greatly changed this. Families no longer look to their immed-iate neighbours for their social life; the street loyalties of the slums do not transplant to the new housing areas, and men no longer have to live near the factories where they work, as miners on the whole still do. Children, also, are now being conveyed long distances, both in town and country, to their schools. None the less until human beings grow wings, and even if petrol makes their leg muscles flabby, neighbourhood

will still be meaningful. The church and the pub or club within walking distance and geographical neighbours, especially where there are young families, will always condition social life; so that the ecclesiastical parish if its boundaries are sensible will continue to be more than just an ecclesiastical convenience. But the Church must be able to re-shape the parochial pattern, merge parishes, suppress others, and create new ones easily and freely. Old so-and-so or angry young so-and-so cannot be allowed to delay the necessary pastoral change for a generation. It is necessary to bring back into operation and make part of normal ordering the provisions of the Reorganization Areas Measure which enabled diocesan bishops to deal effectively with the situations created by war damage, and which unwisely was ended just when we had to begin to deal with the changes resulting from new building.

Society, today, consists of other groupings than geographical ones – professional, industrial, and vocational. In order to do its pastoral and teaching work, the Church's ministry, ordained and lay, has to be within these groupings – and not only because that is good tactics. Industry has produced a mental climate and outlook just as much as university life has, or the strains and stresses of a hospital (both for staff and patients). The Church not only has to set its 'general practitioners' within these non-parochial groupings, it also needs to have more specialists – and especially men and women who can sustain a lively dialogue with those who are the majority of the population and are to be found on or beyond the Christian frontiers.

The part of the Paul Report which seems to the writer least satisfactory is the sociological survey. It was not a complete picture either of the Ministry or the Church, and in consequence it led to some generalizations and recommendations which would be misleading. To take 1,298 parishes at random and ask the incumbents to answer a large number of questions about their parishes and some very personal ones about themselves produces valuable information, and indeed some very moving revelations, but it does not provide a sufficiently complete picture of an episcopally ordered Church. A complete survey being impracticable, it would have been better to take as a sample, say, five dioceses, different in character, and to invite all the ordained men and full-time workers in them to say their piece – and their bishop as well.

Mr Paul, with warm sympathy, draws out the loneliness of the parson's life, and also the undue isolation of parish and parish. From the nature of his work and his responsibilities a priest or a bishop must to some extent be a lonely man – better so than that he should be a gossip – and that is one argument for married clergy. But he need not be, and should not be, an unfriendly man or piously shut away from normal, healthy social life with its fun and games as well as its serious pursuits and interests. Indeed what we are suffering from most in the ministry is that priests do not stay long enough in a parish to become a part of the community; and that many do not identify themselves with its whole life and are not identified as 'one of us'. This involvement is needful in the urban parish as much as in the rural one. I would risk the generalization that those who complain most of isolation are the isolationists, for a great deal is now being done, certainly in most dioceses, and in areas within dioceses, to bring clergy together and also their wives, which is important, and the women-workers who are often more lonely than the clergy. More no doubt could and should be done. There is need for more experiment in 'team' or group ministries for more cooperation between the parishes in a neighbourhood, including the Free Churches, and sometimes for larger units, and for the sharing of specialists if there are any to share. But having lived and worked in the heavy industrialized areas of England for most of my ministry – and I hope with my eyes open – I find some of the proposals in the Report rather brash. Some, moreover, seem to disregard the distinctive character of an episcopally ordered Church in which the diocese – bishop, clergy, people – is and must always be the Church, a family complete in itself; but not, God forbid, unconcerned or unfriendly towards the other similar units in the national Church and beyond, or towards other Christian groups.

4. *Fitting the right man to the right job*. Mr Paul thinks that both private patronage and the incumbent's freehold hinder this, and would therefore abolish both. He has a strong prejudice against the exercise of patronage by colleges; and thinks that in the hands of party trusts it is as indefensible as nepotism.

It is true that private patrons are being driven by the difficulty of finding men to turn more and more to the bishop, and that much of the time of bishops is occupied with the laborious and unending task of filling livings. This, however, must always be a part of their duty, with the help of their staff, and in ever closer consultation with the representatives of the parish to which an appointment has to be made. Some variety of patronage in a diocese is not without merit, provided the views of a P.C.C. are well considered and the bishop on their behalf has more power than he has at present to refuse to institute. It would certainly be a help in the exercise of patronage if there were for the whole country a well-kept clergy list—more informative than *Crockford* – that all patrons could consult.

One would therefore wish to put a pen through such proposals as a clergy staff board and regional staff boards for all appointments – in theory bureaucratic and in practice unfeasible – and the proposals that all posts should be 'leasehold', which look like a misuse of a difficult legal term, and that incumbencies should be of a more or less fixed duration.

The Christian ministry is an intensely personal thing. It cannot be appraised just by statistics, for X never equals Y in the ordained ministry. No two of us are alike either in our competencies or in our incompetencies. A diocese should be of a size to allow for relaxed and friendly dialogues between the diocesan authority and priests and workers in it – and not too much authority in evidence. And so indeed it often and happily is. This pastoral relationship is far and away the most important part of a bishop's work; and it tends to be obscured in the Church of England by the excessive size of some of the dioceses and the frequency of translations, and it would be still more obscured if 'direction', about which there is a good deal in this Report, was done by boards set up by the Church Assembly, and operating through professional civil service. In an episcopal Church the only 'direction' which is tolerable, even if it is not always perfect, is that of a diocesan bishop. Moreover, the antithesis sometimes made between 'pastoral and administrative' is often exaggerated. Part of a bishop's pastoral care is to ensure that the resources of a diocese are used to help his clergy to have good living and working conditions. A Church can only fulfil its mission in a quarrelsome world when, in its common life, so to say, 'mercy and truth are met together; righteousness and peace kiss each other.' But a bureaucratic re-shaping of our ministry is not the way to achieve happy fellowship to arm it for its unremitting warfare in the world.

The proposals of the Report concerning the tenure of benefices are also too bureaucratic. The Curé d'Ars would have had a poor time and would have probably missed canonization if the Paul Report had operated in France in the nineteenth century. How long a man should stay in a living depends on delicately poised considerations – the man's character, gifts, and sense of vocation, the nature of the parish and his relationship with the people in it, the need for his services elsewhere. As bishop, one has sometimes pressed a man to move to another post for which he had the qualifications; and for reasons which did him credit and which proved to be good reasons he would not be moved. Some parish priests do their best work in a relatively short number of years; others are built to stay for many, many years and become greatly beloved in a community which they have come to love greatly. Such situations in a Christian society are not best resolved by rules and regulations appropriate to a civil service or the defence forces.

On the other hand, there will always be a few cases when a priest ought to be moved. Where it is one of the infrequent cases of serious wrong-doing, this is best done, and usually can be done, by persuasion. Only once during thirty years as an archdeacon in one diocese, and bishop of another, has a wrong-doer been so obdurate that one was powerless until the magistrate put him in jail.

The other situations in which the bishop on behalf of the parishioners should have power to move a man are those of a stubborn misfit who insists on staying because he dislikes his people or of a man mentally unbalanced but not certifiable. I recollect a little man living alone many years ago in the wilds of Northumberland and occupying only one room in a large cold parsonage house. There was little furniture in the room and the only colourful thing in it was a large Union Jack covering the pillow-case on his campbed. When I asked him why it was there, he said that it was to keep his head warm. I hadn't the heart to disturb his faith in the efficacy of the national emblem; and I also thought his parishioners might have been more forbearing if they could have seen the pitiful conditions in which he was existing. None the less the situation admittedly was not an argument for the freehold. The remedy for these occasional and sad situations is not rules about length of tenure and courts of inquiry, but the kind of relaxed conversation that is possible in a diocese small enough for the clergy to know, care for, and encourage one another and a family spirit deepens with the years and the bishop may truly be a father-in-God.

5. *The ministry of the laity*. There is a good deal in the Report on the ministry of the laity and the training of the laity to exercise it. Some of the talk in the Church of England on this subject—and there is any amount of it at the present time— would make good Free Churchmen smile. The best service a layman can give is to be an intelligent Christian who tries to express his faith in and through his secular job and in its human relationships, as well as in his private and family life. If he has some leisure for specifically 'church work' there is much he could do according to his gifts. While the shortage of clergy continues and the Church continues to be reluctant to

use women fully, it would immensely strengthen the impact of the Church on society, if in an urban parish the laity between them had a sort of pastoral responsibility for a street or a block and kept the priest informed about this and that. But it is not a lay clerisy that is wanted – a sort of parson in plain clothes out of doors and with a clerical voice in church. In the Industrial Mission in Sheffield we used to say – and they still say – that the function of the priest-missioner was to be a catalyst among a group of workers or managers, and it was these who had to make contact and enter into dialogue with their fellows. In administration, competent laymen and women, accustomed to affairs, can give the Church valuable service at every level; but one has to confess that often clergy are unduly fearful about entering into this sort of partnership; and one wonders why, for in my experience busy and influential laymen have been ready to serve in this way provided they are given responsibility and are not expected just to be yes-men, with a parson always in the chair.

6. *The training and direction of the ministry.* Although Mr Paul's report is to the Council for the Ministry he has not much to say about its primary business. What the Church is doing, or not doing, in regard to its ordinands is a matter in debate. Rightly or wrongly the bishops delegated much of their responsibility to a Central Advisory Council. That Council has been becoming increasingly executive and the dominating influence in it has tended to be those who have a vested interest in the existing forms of training. During the last forty years there has been a growing separatedness between the clergy and laymen and women. One reason for this is the smaller proportion of ordinands who have been to a university (and this at a time when the number of universities and students in them is increasing greatly). A second reason is the kind of training being given. In my young days many university graduates were ordained without going on to a theological college, if they satisfied a bishop's examining chaplains – William Temple for one. Nowadays, virtually all ordinands have to spend two or three years segregated in a

theological college. An intelligent man who has been to a university and entered fully into its corporate life can survive this discipline very often to his profit, even if sometimes the intellectual life and teaching are far from stimulating and the examination for which he has to study is open to criticism. But the effect on many non-university men, especially young men who are not mentally vigorous, of reading theology and residing in a community entirely of ordinands is often prejudicial to their ministry afterwards. As a rule men ought to study theology alongside men and women going into other walks of life, and have to enter into dialogue with them. If their experience of life is limited then they should get some on the shop floor of industry and the like, or by studying in another country. The training before ordination should be more varied, and for some more specialized, and also more related to contemporary thought and life. We want an English equivalent of the Mission de France, which gives men an intensive training to serve in the de-Christianized areas in town and country, and keeps in touch with them after they go out and brings them back from time to time for long 're-fresher courses' – easier to do with a celibate priesthood. Mr Paul argues cogently that ordinands as a condition of being grant-aided should accept 'direction' for the first five years of their ministry, presumably from the bishop who ordains and licences them in consultation with their theological college principal and afterwards with his chaplains. I say 'presumably' because the Report seems to regard a diocesan bishop as a species of ecclesiastical dignitary, and therefore argues that in equity if the clergy should have a so-called leasehold, terminable after a defined period, so should bishops. But in a Church catholic and episcopal, the Bishop is not just a dignitary or a district superintendent or a father-in-God *in vacuo*. A bishop is, or should always be, the bishop of a see.* If it no longer is practicable that he should as it were be married to his see till death them part, as in the primitive Church, and as it still is in the Orthodox Churches, it would make non-

* See above, pp. 73f.

sense of episcopacy if they were divorced by the fiat of a Church Assembly. There is a point in the ordering of a Church where doctrine as well as convenient practice has to be taken into account.

Finally, Mr Paul's comprehensive survey has firm words about the age of retirement and pensions. Here, also, the analogy of the civil service cannot be pressed. A civil servant ceases to be a civil servant when he retires; and may become a company director, a gentleman of leisure, or both; but a priest remains a priest and a bishop a bishop. With a shortage of clergy running into thousands the Church needs to give serious thought how best to use the whole or part-time service of men entitled to a pension at seventy, and ready for less-exacting charges. It would be wasteful, not of money, but of talent, wisdom and spirituality, if they were just given free or inexpensive accommodation in a reservation in Worthing or some such place. Those who revere the memory of Baron von Hügel will recall how much he owed – and others also – to the spiritual direction of Abbé Huvelin who for years was a fragile, supernumerary priest in a large parish in Paris.

Mr Paul's report which was well received by the Church Assembly, is in the best sense controversial, and will certainly draw opposition from those who temperamentally hate a new idea when they are compelled to see it. It is to be hoped that the recommendations which are unsuited to an episcopal Church, or are of less value, will not distract attention from those which must be carried out for the good of Church and people so that the one may be re-invigorated to fulfil its Christian mission to the other.

NOTES

1. This chapter is slightly altered from an article which appeared in the *Quarterly Review*, in July 1964, and is reprinted by kind permission of the editor, Sir John Murray, K.C.V.O.

2. *The Deployment and Payment of the Clergy*. A report by Leslie Paul. Church Information Office, 1964.

3. *Men, Money and the Ministry*. A Plea for Economic Reform in the Church of England. Longmans, Green, 1937. *Putting our House in Order*. Longmans, Green, 1961.

4. Report of the Commission of the House of Bishops, on the remuneration and Housing of the Clergy and matters relating to the Legislative and Administrative Machinery of the Church of England, generally approved by the unanimous vote of the House of Bishops, 20 January 1943. Published as a Church Assembly White Paper, C.A. 719.

5. Queen Anne's Bounty (1704) and the Ecclesiastical Commissioners (1836) were united from April 1948 to form the Church Commissioners. Its officers are listed and its constitution set out on pages 182–4 of the Church of England Year Book.

THE CHURCH OF ENGLAND
AS BY LAW ESTABLISHED –
UNFIT FOR EXPORT?

'WHAT should they know of England who only England know?' The answer is 'very little' and that 'little' almost certainly out of true perspective. The same applies to the Church of England. For no sooner had the sixteenth-century seamen of England started out to claim their share of the new worlds of the Americas, the Indies and Africa, than we find that it was assumed that the Church of England would in some sense 'follow the flag'. The Book of Common Prayer was first used by Drake's ship's company when in 1565 he landed on the coast of California a little north of where San Francisco stands today.

The story of the attempt to export the Church of England as by law established is a curious one, though perhaps not more curious than the attitude of the average Englishman to his national Church!

Any new look at our National Church needs to take into consideration the story of the attempt to export it. The final verdict may be that it was strictly 'not for export'. Yet the attempt was made. And there have been some very unexpected results, which are with us still. The curious will find a brief outline of the story in what follows.

Europe, when at the end of the fifteenth or during the sixteenth centuries it broke out from its restricted boundaries and started to explore the world, was in almost every respect still medieval Europe.

In that old medieval Europe the Church everywhere was 'established'. The constitutional struggles of the Middle Ages were struggles between Church government and civil government within one homogeneous society.

Hence it was that the expansion of Europe, when it came, was at one and the same time the expansion of commerce, government and Christianity. It was in this threefold guise that western civilization made its impact on the rest of the world. An inevitable sequel to this form of expansion was that with the Christianity thus exported went the export of some form of Church establishment. In so far, then, as England was involved in the expansion of Europe it was axiomatic that the Church of England as by law established was fit for export. Such fitness, however much disputed, continued to be assumed for a very long time, down until the middle of the nineteenth century in the minds of many of its protagonists. Curious vestigial remains of this view survived until the middle of the twentieth century! The idea has taken an 'unconscionable time dying', a tribute perhaps to the potency of the medieval dream, to the idea of Christendom.

It was that dream, that idea which made it natural for the explorers and *conquistadors* of Spain and Portugal to seek papal bulls to legitimize their claims to divide between them the fruits of their adventuring. Nor was it conventional piety which led Columbus to declare that the Spanish monarch sent him to the countries of India 'to learn their disposition and the proper method of conveying them to our holy faith'. It was indeed as an 'establishment' that Roman Catholicism was exported to the Americas and to Asia.

In precisely the same way Richard Hakluyt in his *Discourse on Western Planting* published in 1584 could write:

Seeing that the people of that part of America . . . are idolaters . . . it remayneth to be thoroughly weyed and considered by what meanes and by whom this most godly and christian work may be performed of inlarginge the glorious gospell of Christe . . . Nowe the Kinges and Queenes of England have the name of Defenders of the Faithe. By which title I think they are not only chardged to mayneteyne and patronize the faithe of Christe, but also to inlarge and advance the same.

The Letters Patent granted to the Virginia Company in 1606

expressed the hope that the colonization of Virginia would lead to the propagation of Christianity among the Indians. The Levant Company sent out chaplains to the Near East. The charter of 1698 of the English East India Company 'made provision for a Christian minister in each garrison and superior factory of the Company'. It is to be noted that in all these instances the form of church order to be established was assumed to be that of the Church of England. And as late as 1793 Charles Grant, one of the greatest of all the Directors of the East India Company, sought to promote in Parliament a bill which included the clause:

> The Court of Directors . . . are hereby empowered and required to send out, from time to time . . . fit and proper persons . . . as schoolmasters, missionaries; or otherwise . . . The said Court of Directors are hereby empowered and required to give directions to the governments in India to settle the destination and to provide for the necessary and decent maintenance of the persons so to be sent out.

This clause was deleted from the bill. But the opposition to the inclusion of this clause was in no way based on any objection to the export of 'establishment' as such. The services of chaplains had always been welcomed by the company provided their activities were confined to the personnel of the company. What was greatly feared was the influx of missionaries to work among the general population. When, therefore, in 1813 a bill was passed through Parliament to compel the Company to legalize the entry of missionaries into India it did so, as it were, under the provision for the appointment of a bishop. There was, in 1813, says Charles Grant's most recent biographer, 'no great resistance to the idea of creating an ecclesiastical establishment in India', though this was not how Wilberforce and others read the situation.

There is, nevertheless, something ironical about some words of the then Bishop of Chester (Bishop Law) which occur in his valedictory address to Bishop Middleton immediately before he sailed for India in 1814:

The establishment of Episcopacy (*in India*) will most effectually check every erroneous doctrine, stop the wild progress of enthusiasm and spread the knowledge of uncorrupted Christianity.

He certainly believed that the Church of England, by law established, was fit for export. Many still agreed with him. Meanwhile, however, four factors had been operating to change men's minds, and to call in question the whole concept of Christendom as a united society living under one law and accepting the authority of one Church.

The claim of national governments, the heirs of the Middle Ages, to establish by law one form of the Christian religion to the exclusion of all else was first challenged by the rise of dissent. As far as England was concerned, whatever disabilities dissenters and Roman Catholics might continue to suffer, the issue was settled by the revolution of 1688. Only the inveterate conservatism of a still predominantly rural society, and the rule of an unreformed Parliament could maintain the exclusive privileges of the Church establishment well into the nineteenth century.

A second decisive influence was the revolt of the American Colonies. Here dissent had from the first been politically powerful. The first Amendment to the Federal Constitution of the U.S.A. settled the issue with the words:

Congress shall make no law respecting an establishment of religion,

which restriction was, in the Fourteenth Amendment, extended to the State legislatures.

A third factor which influenced the North American scene in both the U.S.A. and Canada, and which provided the impetus for the secularization of increasing areas of life in nineteenth-century Britain, was the French Revolution with its attack upon all forms of privilege. This is the real watershed between the Middle Ages and the modern world. Although fierce rear-guard actions were fought to insist that the Church of England as by law established could be exported, these were all defeated by the middle of the nineteenth century, and the attack was launched on the very principle of establishment in England itself.

But another movement of thought, which probably had as signal an effect on men's minds as the other three influences, was in part an expression of those influences in the field of economics. A 'nation of shopkeepers' began, in the last quarter of the eighteenth century, to call in question the politico-economic policy of the two previous centuries. Under the influence of Adam Smith, of the experience of the revolt of the American Colonies, and of the expansion of British power in India, the idea of free trade triumphed over the old mer-cantilist theories of protection and of political control. It is not too fanciful to see in the separation of Church and State an ecclesiastical equivalent of the economic doctrine of free trade. The nineteenth century became the century in which, on many very different and sometimes contradictory grounds, the minds of men moved away from a belief in a religious 'establishment' by law, in favour of a pluralist society.

It was, however, by no means self-evident to all men in the nineteenth century that the Church of England, as by law established, could not be exported in the modern world, but must make way for something very different indeed which we call Anglicanism. The influence of the earlier idea has indeed continued, in some places down to the present day.

Three curious illustrations of this may be cited whose repercussions, in some cases for evil, in some cases for good, are with us still.

In Canada the Constitutional Act of 1791 set aside 2,400,000 acres, or 3,750 square miles, of some of the finest land in Canada for the benefit of the 'Protestant Clergy'. The author of a recent study 'Church and State in Canada West' comments:

To whom did this munificent patrimony belong, or more exactly who were the Protestant Clergy? No definition of the term was included in the Constitutional Act, and for half a century after the creation of Upper Canada, thanks to the efforts of the Right Reverend John Strachan and the collusion of successive colonial governors, the Church of England retained a monopoly of the Reserves.[1]

The most cursory study of Church and State relations in Canada during this period demonstrates the importance of this issue. Bishop John Strachan of Toronto was the storm centre of a controversy which gravely divided both Church and State in Canada. Despite the fact that members of the Church of England were in a minority he insisted, and successfully insisted for many years, that the monopoly of the reserves belonged to the Church of England. And he was quite clear that the Church of England in Canada and the Church of England in England were one and the same establishment.

An attempt was made to solve the bitter dispute on the basis of dividing the reserves so that the Church of England would receive 25 per cent, the Church of Scotland 25 per cent and the rest to be divided between such other denominations as were recognized by the law of Upper Canada. Bishop Strachan described this proposal as being:

as injurious to the established Church as it is repugnant to the 31st of Geo. 3rd Chap. 31, (*The Constitutional Act of* 1791) and the fundamental principles of the British Constitution. By this bill the national church would be robbed of nearly three quarters of her patrimony, British birthright would be destroyed, error, schism and dissent would be promoted by levelling the 'clergy' to the status of dissenting ministers, and the cause of Protestantism would be endangered.[2]

The bishop exhorted his followers not to fear the provincial legislature 'but lift your eyes unto England from whence alone could come worldly salvation'. And the Parliament in England went a very long way towards justifying his exhortation. In 1840 this attempt of the Canadian legislature to solve the problem was annulled. A fresh settlement ordered that the Church of England, whose members constituted approximately 20 per cent of the population, should receive 42 per cent of the reserves, and the Church of Scotland which was almost equal in number to the Church of England receive 21 per cent, while the rest of the Protestants who numbered nearly half the population received 38 per cent divided among them.

Only in 1854 was the issue finally settled by the Canadian Parliament on a commutation basis. And the essence of the solution was the final separation of Church and State.

A second illustration may be cited from India. The Charter renewed by Parliament to the East India Company in 1813 laid the foundation of the Church establishment in India by providing for the appointment of a bishop and three archdeacons.

The Letters Patent for the consecration of Bishop Middleton, the first bishop, issued on May 2 1814, instructed the Archbishop of Canterbury as follows:

Make the bishop and his successors subordinate to the archiepiscopal see of Canterbury in the same manner as any diocesan bishop in England. . . . Authorize the bishop to exercize his episcopal functions within the limits of his see and to exercize spiritual and ecclesiastical jurisdiction, personally or by his commissaries, according to the ecclesiastical laws of England; to license all ministers and chaplains to officiate within his diocese according to the rites and liturgy of the Church of England.

Whether we study the old charters providing for the appointment of chaplains, or consider the later Acts and Letters Patent creating bishoprics, there can be no doubt that it was the intention of Parliament to set up an institution in India which was identical with the Church of England.

It is further to be noted that the Charter Act of 1813 stated that the salaries of the bishop and the three archdeacons, in addition to the company's chaplains, were to be paid out of the revenues of the three Presidencies, Bengal, Madras and Bombay.

When in 1858 the British Government took over all political control from the East India Company it also took over the financial responsibilities for the Church establishment. And these responsibilities included the maintaining out of public funds of all the churches built by the East India Company, not to mention those to be built by the government.

An intriguing comment occurs in a book written in 1859 on the subject of Christianity in India, which reads:

Whether consistently with strict justice a Christian government can support its own church out of revenues derived from Hindu and Mahommedan tax payers may be an open question.

The question remained open! When in 1927 the Church of India, Burma and Ceylon achieved its independence from Canterbury the following clauses were embodied in the Act:

The maintenance of certain churches and chaplains by the Secretary of State shall be continued after severance. . . . That the position of chaplains, appointed and paid out of government revenues, shall be retained under any change of constitution.[3]

Perhaps the most curious of these illustrations of the persistent attempts to export the idea of the 'establishment' of the Church of England is to be found in the all-pervasive influence of Dr Arnold on the English public schools. These schools, with very few exceptions, were in their religious complexion, either explicitly or implicitly Church of England in their ethos. Furthermore it was from these schools that the 'Third British Empire' in the main recruited its administrators, its governors, and the directors of its educational and medical services. What is perhaps as important, in the sequel, is that it was from the same public schools that there came many of the missionaries who were raised to the overseas episcopate, or who were sent out from this country to be bishops of missionary dioceses.

The only qualification needed to the above generalization is the acknowledgement of the fact that a substantial minority of those who held office in the imperial episode were members of the Church of Scotland. But the fact that they were themselves, also, members of an established Church, in practice, reduced the significance of this qualification. They shared with those from south of the border a certain understanding of the principle of an establishment of religion.[4]

Arnold's great aim was to turn out gentlemen who were Christians. It is easy to quarrel with that as an all-embracing objective for an educational system, but in the very wide and deep sense in which he interpreted this objective Arnold did succeed in setting a distinctive stamp upon the products of the English public-school system. The time is not yet when anything like justice can be done to the men who ruled India and the colonial empire. What is possible is to see how this educational pattern did in fact influence the Church–State relationship in British territories overseas where the Church of England was certainly not established by law.

For a clear understanding of the situation between 1840 and 1940 in the colonial dependencies of Britain it has to be remembered that the overseas dioceses were at first missionary dioceses directly under the jurisdiction of the Archbishop of Canterbury. Only since 1945 has the rapid development of autonomous Provinces overseas led to the wholesale abandonment of this jurisdiction. From 1840–1940 virtually every overseas diocese, jurisdictionally related to Canterbury, was dependent for its episcopate and its expatriate clergy upon the man-power of the Provinces of Canterbury and York, supplemented in some degree from the other Provinces in the British Isles.

This dependence was a precise complement to the dependence of the colonial service for recruitment from the same area. What is significant is that what both had in common was education in English public schools.

There was, therefore, an 'old school tie' nexus between missionary and district officer, between bishop and governor, which undoubtedly served in many cases to create for the Church of England in the area concerned a privileged position. Nor can it be doubted that this relationship did, in fact, serve to facilitate many a mission programme. This can be stated without in anyway impugning either the integrity of the political officers or questioning their proper neutrality in matters of common interest to Christians of other churches. Nor is it to be assumed that bishops and other missionaries abused their position to extort privileges for themselves. It stands to reason, however, that where a man *qua* bishop has a background and tradition in common with another man who is a government official, a good deal of business can be discharged between the two 'outside office hours'. Nor is there anything more sinister in this than in the comparable fact that as much of the government of England is determined over the dinner table as in the Houses of Parliament.

In the sequel in many of Britain's colonial territories in the period under consideration the Church of England acquired a strictly unofficial but *de facto* position as a quasi-establishment. That is a statement which it could never be easy to document. But it is only necessary to read the biographies of government officials and of overseas bishops, to study the reports of Commissions and to notice the persons giving evidence before them, as well as to know something of how the British Colonial Empire was governed, to see that there is substance in this suggestion of a quasi-establishment. In a sense it was an inevitable sequel to Dr Arnold's influence, as well as a sequel to the very long mutual involvement of Church and State in English history.

There is on record an interesting letter from a former pupil of Dr Arnold's, John Philip Gell, who as a schoolmaster in Tasmania was prompted to try to secure his old headmaster as Bishop of the Diocese. Writing to a friend Gell said:

I wrote lately to the Colonial Office to move them if possible to get a certain Bishop 'magnanimous enough to comprehend and hold fast the noble sentiment that the state is Christ's – which the Principles of the Church of England contain – liberal enough to alter and adapt the forms embodying those principles to the condition of a new colony; independent enough to shake off the trammels of the age and still keep a steady line of conduct.[5]

That letter describes a certain kind of man, holding certain convictions, which in fact characterized a very considerable number of those who ruled the Colonial Empire as well as those who served it in their capacity as missionaries.

This third illustration is very different in kind from the one chosen from Canada, or the one from India. It may nevertheless be hazarded that it was this third conception of the Church of England overseas which had far and away the greatest influence in forwarding the missionary work of the Church, and not only of the Church of England.

In attempting to make some appraisal of the gains and losses to the Christian cause of the long continued attempt to export the Church of England as by law established, it is necessary to take note of one fundamental fact. The attempt to export the Church of England was not a piece of religious imperialism. Essentially the attempt was born of the conviction that religion is meant to be relevant to every aspect of the life of man. If this is true then whatever be the relations between Church and State there can be no question of attempting a separation between religion and the state. Religion cannot abdicate its responsibility for the whole life of man and remain religion.

There is here a dilemma to which no solution has yet been found, as is demonstrably the case in the United States of America. There, despite the constitutional attempt to 'erect a wall between Church and State', despite the Supreme Court's decision in 1947 in *Everson* v. *Board of Education, 330 US 1* that 'That wall must be kept high and impregnable. We could not approve the slightest breach', the issue is as alive as ever and still engages Americans in passionate debate.

With this fundamental reality of an inescapable tension kept in mind it is possible to summarize certain aspects of gain and loss from the past attempt to export the Church of England, as by law established.

1. Indisputably its relation with the State in England has enabled it to get a preliminary foothold in many parts of the world. And the development of that foothold has not prevented the Church so established from proceeding in due

course to achieve its own independence. Nowhere overseas has this first advantage worked in the long run against the true interest of the Church and its Mission.

Nevertheless it must also be noted that the privileges once claimed on the score of establishment have embittered relations with other churches and made the approach to church unity more difficult. Canada, as illustrated here, is a case in point.

2. The principle of establishment carried with it a certain view of the State, what Philip Gell calls 'the noble sentiment that the State is Christ's'. This affords to those who hold this view, and Gell is surely right in adding that this view is agreeable to the 'principles of the Church of England', the opportunity to claim 'the crown rights of the Redeemer'.

This advantage has been illustrated on countless occasions in the history of Britain's expansion overseas.

Nevertheless it must also be admitted that it can all too easily make for subservience to the State. It has not always been easy for those who have enjoyed a quasi-establishment to find a middle way between protest and obedience.

3. The principle of establishment as understood in England has a definite territorial significance. The bishop, and by delegation the parish priest, has a distinct area of responsibility, and the responsibility is not confined to those of his own religious allegiance but in some sense embraces all those living in the area. This territorial emphasis has latent within it, even if not explicitly expressed, a missionary impetus. The 'established' Church is not a sect ministering exclusively to its own members. It has a concern for 'all sorts and conditions of men'.

This predisposes an established Church to be concerned with its cultural mission as well as with its evangelistic mission. It seeks to influence the community throughout the whole range of human experience. This predisposition has found some reflection in the 'Anglican Churches' which have sprung from the Church of England as by law established. But the experience of being one denomination among many, which is the opposite of 'establishment', had made this wider cultural influence less easy to maintain.

If Erastianism is the peril of a territorial emphasis, introversion is the peril of denominationalism. History suggests that the perils can only be avoided by treating evangelism in its widest understanding as the Church's priority. It would seem that it is in this way that the territorial Church achieves its freedom just as it is through active engagement in evangelism that a denomination finds its way to a larger unity.

There are two questions which may fairly be asked arising out of this brief summary of a very complicated history. The *first* question may be posed thus: 'Can it be said that there is a problem involved in the relationship between the Established Church in England and the other Provinces of the Anglican Communion where the principle of "establishment" does not obtain?'

The *second* question, a subordinate one, might read: 'Does the effect of Establishment in England make some contribution or alternatively offer some kind of disadvantage to the Anglican Communion as a whole?'

It can be confidently asserted that whatever may have obtained in the past there is today no problem created for any autonomous Province of the Anglican Communion by virtue of the fact that the Church in England is 'Established'. The autonomous Provinces are strictly autonomous. They are linked together by certain accepted principles of Faith and Order which are entirely unrelated to any particular relationship with the State. The Archbishop of Canterbury, whatever his position in England, is in relation to the bishops of the Anglican Communion throughout the world *primus inter pares*. He has no jurisdiction. In so far as he may still be a court of appeal in certain cases it is due to the veneration held for the Chair of St Augustine and not for his position as the Primate of an Established Church.

The subordinate question raises a more debatable issue. Much will depend upon how the student of history interprets the role of the Church in relation to the State. The fact that the Church in England is Established does afford many unique opportunities of spiritual service to the nation which are not available in the same degree to Churches which are not established. The Established Church may fail to take these opportunities but they remain as long as the Church is established. From the point of view of the other Province of the Anglican Communion it could be held to be an advantage to have the continual reminder, provided by the Church in England, that the Church has an inescapable relationship to every aspect of human life and an incontrovertible responsibility for doing something about the relationship. Disestablished Churches, lacking any statutory provision for dialogue with the State, can more easily evade the responsibility for a prophetic ministry.

There would appear to be no evidence that the fact that the Church of England is an Established Church works to the present disadvantage of any of the autonomous Provinces of the Anglican Communion, though, as this chapter has indicated, the evidence of past history is ambiguous.

This essay has been concerned to show how some have attempted to export the Church of England by law established. The evidence would seem to suggest that in its historic form it is unfitted for export. But it is no easy task to draw up a balance sheet of the attempt and to assess its success and failure. Perhaps the claim can be made that the very attempt in effect saved the Church of England from being insular while its failure had as its by-product the emergence of the Anglican Communion.

Yet the basic issues of the relations of Church and State are still with us in every country in the world, as much where there is a declared separation of Church and State as when the Church is still established. This must be so for as Christopher Fry makes Becket say to Henry:

> There is a true and living
> Dialectic between the Church and the State
> Which has to be argued for ever in good part.
> It can't be broken off or turned
> Into a clear issue to be lost or won.
> Its the nature of man that argues.

NOTES

1. John S. Moir, *Church and State in Canada West*, University of Toronto Press, 1959, p. 27.

2. John S. Moir, op. cit., p. 34.

3. As late as 1946–7 the expenditure on ecclesiastical affairs shown in the Indian accounts is £285,597.

4. In Kenya, when it was decided that missionaries should be nominated to the Legislative Council to represent 'native interests' following the recommendations of the 1923 White Paper *Indians in Kenya*, 'Only members of the two Churches established in the United Kingdom were so nominated: two from the Church of Scotland, and four from the Church of England'. See *Essays in Imperial Government*, ed. by K. Robinson and F. Madden, Oxford, Basil Blackwell, 1963, p. 145.

5. Quoted in Frances J. Woodward, *The Doctor's Disciples*, Oxford University Press, 1954, p. 102.

WHAT SHOULD BE THE
NEW LOOK?

A variety of factors now combine to focus the attention of the Church on the present Church–State relationship. There is the issue of Crown Appointments. The Anglican-Methodist negotiations must, sooner or later, face the question – and sooner one hopes, rather than later, since it ought to be a matter of major concern for uniting Churches that have held mutually exclusive views on the subject to clarify their minds upon it. Then there is the possibility of embarrassment in the attitude that Parliament might adopt to new canons, and to such new 'freedoms' that the Church might seek for the implementation of reform measures, along the lines of the Paul Report and so on. More potentially explosive, probably, than any of these – though there is no desire, seemingly, in Church or State to light the fuse, is the growing divergence between Church and State law on divorce and remarriage. And always there is the problem of the erosion of the Church with the growing secularization of the nation. There are occasional rumbles, but it is hard to believe that the shift of the nation away from its National Church can allow the constitutional relationship to remain permanently unquestioned.

The danger is that these issues, though important, are calculated to focus the Church–State, Church–Society issue too narrowly, and foster the impression – certainly within the Church – that by itself some adjustment of the Establishment, or even Disestablishment for that matter, might be the crucial issue, or that by themselves, such adjustments could spell new life and liberty for the Church and her mission. It is doubly dangerous in that it can obscure all the deeper problems of the Church in relation to the nation.

The Secularization of Our Society

By far the largest of those problems, posed to the Church certainly, is the growing secularization of society, the numerical shrinking of the Church and her increasingly peripheral relationship to society. One should hasten to add, however, that 'secularization' is not simply to be used as a term of denigration. Though it has many disturbing concomitants that threaten human beings and humane values, it is to be distinguished from 'secularism', a closed and positive, if often unconscious ideology, that does conflict with the Christian faith. Essentially, 'secularization' is a neutral term descriptive of a process that leads to an autonomous human culture, which in the course of its development, breaks with traditional religious axioms and practices in so far as they impose the limitations of a religious world-view. We should note that secularization and the secular axioms of thought make new demands upon the theological thinking of the Church and upon her understanding of 'mission' to a world that is autonomous, and which, if not 'come of age', is certainly 'coming of age'.

The secularization of the nation has been studied in many aspects. It is the consequence of new forms of society and of new human assumptions, themselves largely consequent upon the scientific revolution. Its impact upon religious institutions, practices and assumptions has also been studied in recent years, and those studies have shown the erosion of the Churches, and their steady weakening as formative influences in the national life. The pattern and history of that estrangement differ in the different social groups and classes, and even today the picture is not monochrome across the nation. But steadily the National Church has been weakening – in common with all the 'folk' Churches of European nations, both catholic and protestant. More particularly and significantly, has been that weakening in relation to particular groups such as industrial workers, technologists and managers – who con-

stitute the 'pilot' classes of the new society that has come into
being. The change down the ages has been succinctly put by
Lewis Mumford in his history of urban cultures:

> In the mediaeval city the Church was a dominant: no part of
> life could fail to record its existence and influence. In the great
> 17th century capitals, the Church had become a recessive; still an
> imposing visible presence, but no longer a unifying and dynamic
> social force. In the metropolis today the Church is a survival ... it
> contributes little to the active spiritual life of the city.[1]

However we qualify the impressions of an imposing past –
and they need qualification – and whatever new areas of life
have appeared in the contemporary Church – and there are
many areas of new life – the steps in the transition as Mumford
defines them are not really deniable ... Dominant ... Recessive ... Survival.

The real question – and the question of Establishment – is
about the reaction we make to this changed situation. Our
tears, as our time, are wasted by indulging in nostalgia. Even
less should we hope or wish to reverse the process. And indeed, if we believe that the major structural forces underlying
this development in human history are science, technology,
and the new society erected upon them, we are bound to see
the progress, whatever its consequences, as within the providence and economy of God, through which he beckons
men, whatever the dangers, to a new and higher level of
existence.

The danger is that the Church should fail to see the demands
of God upon her in such an analysis, that she should simply
adapt herself to survive in a weakened position in the national
life, allowing secularization – which has promise – to degenerate into secularism – which spells the diminution and
spiritual impoverishment of men. There are many factors that
do encourage such accommodation to weakness, and which
rationalize a weakened relationship with the nation. They are
at work often quite unconsciously. There is the understandable
impatience with the ambiguities of a Laodicean Church, and

with a nominal Christianity of merely occasional conformity. There is the sheer task of holding the Church together and building it into some kind of community. There is the inevitable preoccupation with money and buildings. Theological positions too have played their part – the emphasis on Liturgy, on 'the Church being the Church', which one feels are in part rationalizations of a weakened position, for there is an inherent tendency of all weakening groups to become inward-looking and to find good reasons for doing so. 'Catholics' and 'Evangelicals', though both have stemmed from traditions that have valued the establishment of religion and folk-churches, have become sectarian in tendency. And always, and most seriously for a National Church, is the incapacity to speak with relevance and power on the complex moral and social issues that have plagued the twentieth century. All these factors have operated, inducing an introverted preoccupation with the Church as an organization, a 'congregationalism', and in places a sheer sect-mentality.

The Dilemma of the National Church

In the face of the historical changes that have taken place, the powerful secularizing forces now at work in society, and the instinctive reactions within the Church, inevitably the 'establishment' of religion, the Church–State relationship and the sense of being a National Church have all tended to fade out of the picture. Perhaps the Church at large has acquiesced in this fading as the easiest way of dealing with a tradition that we sense has become something of an illusion, if not an anachronism. For undoubtedly there is illusion in the inherited concept of a National Church in an increasingly secular society. And undoubtedly there is dilemma about what to do with it.

The Gordian knot could be simply cut by the disestablishment of the Church and radical self-accommodation (perhaps united with other bodies) to her reduced size and significance. Certainly it might lead to structural changes in the organization of the Church, and adaptation of her massive plant appropriate to a Church organized for mission as distinct from maintenance. A complex operation, it has its surface attractions, and if the present illusory situation persists, in the face of growing secularization of the nation and progressive weakening of the Church, faithfulness to her mission as a Church of Christ must compel her to seek a more realistic expression of the actual situation, even though it meant radical disassociation from the nation she is called to evangelize – in the interests of that very mission that is so obscured by the present illusion. Whether the Church of England, with her peculiar ethos, timbre, and tradition could do this, is a matter of some doubt; it would more probably surrender the task of mission in our country to a communion with a more 'heteronomous' tradition, more fitted by its tradition to live as a closed minority in our society.

But for the present, whatever the future may demand, I submit that this simple solution would be a three-fold betrayal. It would constitute an overt act radically un-churching the nation and the bulk of its people – who have, on their part, no deliberate, expressed will to be de-Christianized. The nation may be deeply secularized, but is *victim* of the secular forces surely, rather than open-eyed, conscious and determined *agent* of those forces. This can be cogently evidenced, and it is a fact of the greatest importance for a National Church. Again, it would be betrayal of the calling of the Church in the nation, which though it might live as a 'mutation', a sect, in a secular and even hostile society, ought to aim at embodiment within the total life of society, to be woven into its fabric. Certainly this has been the mind of all mainstream Christian traditions and emphatically of the Church of England which has no ethos for sectarianism, and would probably, as we have considered, destroy her very nature in the process. And thirdly, even though the Church of England cannot accept the total responsibility for the mission to England, history has thrown upon her the special responsibility for the *character* of the Christianity that obtains in England. Whatever criticisms can be laid against her – and they are many – it can be asserted, taking the historic view, that liberality of mind, of scholarship and acceptance of new learning – however they have struggled in some periods for existence – have been among her characteristics. It is not unimportant for the country that amongst all the cultural influences that go to make up its 'feel', the Christianity of England should continue to have these characteristics. It is a pity that there is so little awareness of the significant role that religion plays in the formation of those complex things we call the national character, and the character of the nation.

So we see the acute dilemma of the Church of England – bound to the national life by millions of nominal ties, frail and brittle filaments, augustly symbolizing a substance largely in ruins – yet by her calling unable to contract out of the situation into an episcopal sect, and yet on the other hand, if she takes Christianity seriously, neither able to go on living in the illusion of what Sören Kierkegaard called 'geographical Christianity'. Is this dilemma resolvable? That is the major question the Church should be facing. It can be dissected. Do we simply continue in the illusion? Do we seek to accommodate the Church to its reduced position? Or do we make a supreme effort to justify a National Church and the establishment by law of the Christian religion?

A 'Depth' Meaning of Establishment

What is the essential meaning of the Establishment of the Christian religion? What is it in theory, and what is it not? The great classical statements of Hooker or the constitutional definitions do not help us much, partly because they were cast in a pre-democratic period of our history, and partly because they were ratifications of a Church–State, Church–community relationship that existed at a particular time in English history quite different to our own. Unless we throw the whole concept away, we have the task of giving some contemporary meaning and a 'depth' content to these terms if we are to be rid of illusion and grasp the idea of what a genuine Establishment might mean for our period of history.

It is not theocracy – the subjection of State and community to a 'heteronomous' Church standing apart and over against them – which is the 'sect' church writ large. It is not Erastianism, the dumb subservience of a formal state religion to its master. Nor is it the sharp separation of Church and State, Church and society; it is therefore not mere permissiveness or concordat, a bargaining about the conditions of existence or coexistence. Least of all should we allow it to be a mere historical survival of picturesque and ceremonial symbolism. A symbol is empty and confusing unless it is an effective symbol, expressive of a reality, something meaningful and substantial, or at least expressive of a genuine desire that it should represent a reality.

It is harder to say positively what it might mean in our present form of society. Indeed we have to struggle to work out what it can mean, and then struggle to secure it. But certainly we can say that it implies a consciously accepted dynamic relationship between Church and State, between Church and society, based upon the expressed desire of the majority of the nation to subscribe to the Christian faith (however confused the understanding of that faith must often inevitably be), to value it as representing the best that it knows in terms of the truth about life; and to desire that its way of life should be scrutinized by that understanding. However far the nation, and we its people, should fall below what it has expressed as its desire, such consciously-accepted dynamic relationship is still a possibility. The 'marriage' does not allow either spouse to expect perfection of the other!

There is no inherent impossibility of a democracy evolving in a Christian tradition and inheriting a Church–State, Church–community relationship expressing the desire that such a relationship should exist, though from the State's angle, there will no doubt be stronger emphasis on the moral and social aspects of Christianity than on the strictly religious and doctrinal. At least where such a formal expression of desire has come down from the past, only the expressed will of the nation should allow the Church to acquiesce in the rejection of that relationship. Certainly that rejection has not been made. This was the view that William Temple came to hold – and it is not wholly without significance for this thesis, that the last years of his primacy found the nation engaged in a lonely struggle, with little sense of crusade, but nonetheless defending values that find their sanction in a Christian view of what is right.

The Church has the duty to say these things in no uncertain terms. But it is also the responsibility of the Church, in dynamic relationship with the State and with society, to give substance and content to that relationship. That is what 'Establishment' means, and this is the real issue facing the National Church – whether Christianity can be 'established' in the sense of being 'rooted in' the life of the nation, 'securely accepted', 'organizationally related to' society. The actual word carries these very meanings. Other Christian communions have part in this of course; some may make their contribution in close association with the Church of England, in ecumenical relationship, or even within a new Church of England, consequent upon a new 'religious settlement of England' that might be devised. But be that as it may, the National Church has the paramount responsibility to seek that dynamic and creative relationship.

It requires a policy and strategy of engagement with the whole range of national life. Quite simply that. And this means a revolution in the mind and temper of the Church from top to bottom. It requires overall policy and planning, thinking of a high order, a new orientation of training for our clergy, skilful and sensitive instruments forged for engaging the institutions of our pluralist society, not just to strengthen the institution of the Church (which could be a very 'heteronomous' and questionable undertaking utterly opposed to the spirit of genuine Establishment), and all tested by their capacity to throw up and multiply an informed laity, unselfconsciously Christian, in all walks of life. For this is the flower and the most authentic expression of a genuine establishment of Christianity in the life of the nation. It is easy to use the vocabulary of engagement, and to persuade ourselves that this is in fact what we are seeking to do. But to do this in very fact, with honesty, is a massive operation when the weight of the inherited structure and outlook of the Church is conducive to a policy of defensive maintenance.

The Church has of course continuously to win that relationship. In a secular and democratic society 'come of age' she can claim no *right* to be engaged. In a free and open society, that right has to be *earned*. It has to be *won*. She should be helped and encouraged by knowing that where she devises appropriate instruments of engagement there are remarkable opportunities for initiative by the Church, many doors that can be opened, many dialogues established – far more perhaps than she realizes. It by no means follows that such possibilities will always exist. Those initiatives were ruled out in the past by the rigidity of society and the stereotyped alignments of its different social groups, as also by the Church's own rigidity of posture in the national life. They may well decline in the years ahead as secularization advances. It is possible that but an interim period exists, in one of unprecedented social change and considerable moral confusion. But it is no question of the Church being merely 'opportunist', but of rendering her proper service and duty to the life of the nation. It is the thesis of this essay that unless that happens what we do with an Establishment formula is a trivial, tinkering matter, neither here nor there.

A Strategy of Engagement

It is not possible in an essay to spell out in all its possible detail, the range and shape of engagement, and the tactics required of a National Church in our modern society. Indeed, it would itself require a large symposium and still leave much research and experimentation to be done. But we know enough to set out the main areas of engagement in a kind of master plan. There are clearly two main areas in which engagement has to take place: there is the local, territorial, parochial area, and there is the complex area of institutional and social structures – to each of which we proceed to give consideration.

The local church serving the local area will always be the basic ground-floor plan of the Church, and we have inherited such a plan in England in the parish system. Whatever changes may take place in the face of urban redevelopment, group ministries, major parishes, and new boundaries, this will remain the basic structure of the Church. But it needs to become a missionary structure served by a missionary strategy. It needs to shed both illusion and downright error. There is the illusion that stems from an age of religious conformity – that it can simply survive as 'parish church', owned by the parish, used by and caring for all the parish – a lovely ideal, that still embodies a deep truth, but which is utterly unrealistic in the face of the intractable missionary situation, in which the contemporary Church is placed. But on the other hand, it must not become a congregational body, a gathered Anglican sect, or even less as so many people assume, a building to which people 'go' for 'services'. All these assumptions are current, and persist despite a generation of preaching on the Church as the Body of Christ. Alas, that our practice has been a more potent education than our preaching; we tell the people that the Church is not a building – but nearly all our energies and hopes tell us that it is!

These inadequate views will persist until we have a *missionary structure of the local congregation, and a missionary strategy in the parish.* The fact is that the structure of the Church we have inherited was not devised for a missionary situation, but for a pastoral service of a conformist society. Hence the large building at the centre of the parish for public worship and common prayer. In the urban areas with heavy populations this theory and structure have never worked effectively from the beginning; even less so, as the nation has become increasingly urbanized and secularized. The fact is that the local church has to become a missionary movement that engages the parish – banal words that somehow must come to denote something real and tangible. And there are no simple short cuts to such activation of the church – through liturgical changes (important as it may be to make worship simpler, less verbose, more honest), through more clergy even (unless they are ministers of a missionary structure), through some manipulation of the parson's freehold, or more activities of the parish. None of these things by themselves can make up for the lack of a missionary structure of the parish. How might that be secured?

First we require an *attitude of mind* that can combine the doing of two things that have a natural tendency to exclude one another – a difficult operation therefore. We have to combine a 'parish' sense with a 'membership' sense. The former by itself is too weak to hold an effective Christian community together in a secular and mobile society, or to induce a sense of concern and responsibility in those within the church for those outside. The latter by itself tends to the character of a private club and a sect. At present we combine the weaknesses of both without the strengths of either. That is to say, we need a strongly committed membership within the local church of adults, and surely young adults too, who have deliberately contracted-in to the service of the Christian *mission* – as distinct from simply a church – membership or attendance. They would constitute a *movement* – however many or however few – committed to the engagement of the parish in an ongoing, permanent way. Such a committed cadre would be genuinely ministerial, concerned to do something in the parish, unostentatious (no societies or badges!), faithful in a task without being self-consciously 'good churchmen', meeting together apart from the larger congregation only for hard thinking and planning of their work. Only such men and women – and young men and women – can make the parish come alive. Let us think of some of the different roles they would fulfil.

Some would deliberately, but positively and naturally, take their part within the wide range of community activities, in social and political life, according to their bent, capacity, proper interest and situation, but conscious of a dimension to their understanding of life, and with a responsibility and care that spring from an intelligent Christian faith that is related to all secular life. Others would seek the role of 'self-appointed public characters', to use an interesting phrase of Jane Jacobs writing in a very different but relevant context of how community life might be grown in the 'lonely crowd' of the great American cities. In the parish, they would be, to use some of my own phrases, 'points of encounter', and 'centres of infection, affection, and disaffection' – inviting and gathering together informal groups of people, to think and talk, to look at public and social issues large and small and to seek a responsible and Christian judgement. In such ways is Christian truth inductively communicated. We desperately need to discover and equip some laymen for this kind of role. And others would be trained for more purely pastoral work in the parish, supportive of individuals and families with some kind of need or disability, through friendly and useful visitation and neighbourliness. This too is a deep need in our vast urban, mass society, and has its own way of communicating the meaning of Christianity. Indeed all these different kinds of lay action contribute to the health and wholeness of our society; they are intrinsically self-authenticating, but they also communicate Christian faith. The Kingdom of God is about such things happening in our midst.

Perhaps there is little novel in such proposals. Already, by the grace of God, they happen. But they are rarely related to the Church's mission or consciously devised and planned as a normal part of the Church's mission to the world. But just because they do happen, just because such laymen and women do exist, we know what has to be done. There are projects in the contemporary church that come to the edge of being such a missionary movement but fail to realize their promise. Perhaps a defective understanding of the Church's mission to the world is responsible; perhaps a lack of adequate planning or vision. 'Stewardship' campaigns for example, make a step towards it but invariably stop at the very point where they should be passing on to nurture and involve the people that have contracted to contribute to the parish church. Street-warden schemes also have the promise of engagement, but rarely establish more than an information service for the incumbent. And house-meetings, which have a considerable history, have never become structured except in a few outstanding parishes: too quickly they have sought to become 'churches', or they have been held for church-members in the Lenten season, or they have simply been tried and given up. None of these movements has led to an ongoing movement and structure of engagement, built into the parish life, led by a cadre of the laity. (As I have pointed out in other writing – and as indeed should be well known, only Methodism deliberately set out to produce this kind of basic structure – back in the eighteenth and nineteenth centuries – though it was to serve the purpose of nurture rather than engagement. Would that contemporary Methodism were able to bargain such a structure for taking episcopacy into its system!)

There is good reason to believe that the missionary structure of the local church, in the parish or the group of parishes is a possibility. Indeed we know it from what is happening in many areas where a concerted missionary policy has been adopted by the parish. It is a hard operation to orientate the congregation to the world of the parish, to engage the parish on its own territory, and for its own sake – and not merely in order that there should be quick return to the church. And there are conditions if it is to happen in a widespread and continuing way. It needs to be built into diocesan policy with diocesan leadership, and sustained in the parishes notwithstanding the movement of clergy, though one suspects that clergy would stay longer in their parishes if they felt themselves deeply involved in a coherent plan of mission throughout the diocese. It would mean therefore a much closer cooperation of diocese and parish, or to put it another way, parish policy should reflect diocesan policy and the policy of the whole Church. Such a policy of course brings to the fore both clergy and lay training and the closer cooperation of clergy and laity in a common task. Without doubt such a missionary movement in the parish provides immense scope for the laity to be the Church in the world, allowing them to grow up and give that leadership that only they can give – rescuing them from the tedium and triviality of much church life. The Church has new heart and courage, and her faith is renewed, where she becomes a missionary movement, engaging the wider life of the parish. It promises immense encouragement and stimulation to the parish clergy.

A Ministry to the Institutions of Society

Basic though the territorial, parochial structure of the Church has always been, the mission and ministry of the National Church may not be limited to this ground-floor level. She has also sought to exercise a ministry to 'principalities and powers', and her hierarchical structure has geared into the structure of the 'powers that be'. That close nexus of the Church with the 'powers that be' goes far back behind the Tudor settlement. From the sixth century it was inherent in the conversion of a kingdom consequent upon the baptism of a king. The Middle Ages saw the Church a major estate of the nation, providing its educated *élite*, and sacral kingship the highest symbol of that relationship. The spate of Churches at the Reformation, on the basis of *cuius regio eius religio* could not have happened without this integral relationship, and in England the Elizabethan Settlement gave it constitutional definition. It has survived the stresses and strains of political and social revolution, and persists, magnificently if somewhat irrelevantly, into the new secular society of our day.

It is important to note that that close nexus with the 'powers that be', whatever the ambiguities in the relative roles of Church and Caesar, was conceived as part of the Church's mission to the world. Notwithstanding the reactions of radical fringe sects, from the fourth century, mainstream Christianity in all its traditions has sought this organic relationship with the 'powers that be,' and the culture that produced them, as part of her mission to the world. The synthesis of Christ and culture has belonged to her genius whatever compromise and sociological imprisonment 'acculturation' entailed. Certainly without it 'Christendom' would not have existed, nor in our own country that vague, ambiguous, yet real thing we call the 'Christian tradition'. The fact is that the 'baptism' of society is not to be exhausted in, or simply equated with, the aggregate of the baptized in a nation, but requires in addition, this organic relationship of the Church with the corporate institutions of society, the 'principalities and powers' that determine so powerfully the character and feel of a nation, its problems and its possibilities, and the outlook, hopes and fears, and very lives of ordinary people. This relationship with the institutions of society is not wholly dependent upon an Establishment of religion, but it is most certainly contained in the concept of Establishment. This is abundantly evident in the Church–State relationship in England, but the tragedy is that it is restricted in a purely ceremonial and formal way to the principalities of ancient days. One of Hooker's arguments for a range of rank amongst ministers of the Church was that princes and the nobility might 'be matched in a kind of equal yoke' with those from whom they received counsel. And indeed, the Church did give counsel to princes even if some lost their heads in the doing of it! Looking back over English history, Hooker can assert that 'Bishops were wont to be men of great learning in the laws, both civil and of the Church; and while they were so, the wisest men in the land for counsel and government were Bishops'.[2] This was the ministry to principalities and powers, to institutions and corporations, and no one will deny its mark.

Once the significance of this relationship is grasped – and it is a serious commentary on the changed relationship of the

Church to society that so few do grasp it – it is transparently clear that a strategy of engagement of a National Church must take cognizance of a very complex social and organizational structure of our new society, urban, planned, scientific, technological and industrial, its new power groups and *élites*, its maze of new social agencies, and so on. The new 'principalities and powers' might be analysed thus:

- National Government, Ministries, political parties.
- Local Government and municipal officers.
- Industrial organizations; commercial, business and professional bodies of industry.
- Trades Unions, Trades Councils, their area and national structures.
- Universities, Further Education and Technical Colleges, Schools, Education Administration.
- Professional, learned and corporate bodies.
- Social agencies of the Welfare State, national and regional.
- Cultural groups, the Press, the mass media of communication, the arts.
- Voluntary bodies of many kinds.

and so on. . . .

What does engagement of the Church with such a complex of institutions and social organizations entail? First, of course, that Christian men and women should serve in them. Great numbers do, by their vocation and by hard economic necessity. They are the Church in such places. But it is no disrespect to the laity to say that they need far more support than the Church gives them if they are to make the most creative contribution to their secular callings. Teilhard de Chardin addresses magnificent words to the laity of the Church: 'Try with God's help, to perceive the connexion which binds your labour with the building of the Kingdom of God. . . . Why should there not be men vowed to the task of exemplifying, by their lives, the general sanctification of human endeavour, whose common religious ideal would give a full and conscious explanation of the divine possibilities or demands which any wordly occupation implies – men, in a word, who would devote themselves, in the fields of thought, art, industry, commerce and politics, etc., to carrying out in the sublime spirit these demands, the basic tasks which form the very bonework of human society?'[3] These are fine words indeed, but the actualization of such a vision of the Church in the world calls for provision for hard thinking, of lay training, study material, extra-murals, far beyond the provision that is generally made for Christian edification, or even can be made within the confines of the single parish. Christian education, slanted to the problems of men and women in their social and professional lives is a high priority in the engagement of the Church with the institutions of society, *because the Church in the world is the laity*.

But engagement also requires specific projects and instruments of the Church, *qua* Church, to relate to many of these institutions, of which precedents and promises exist in such initiatives as Industrial Mission, University Chaplaincies and many other less established projects. But compared with the whole range of social institutions they are few and in relation to the immense scale of many of them, they are generally inadequate. They are largely the result of individual initiative, with little support from the Church as such, with few resources, and often therefore no more than tokens. Some, just because they have happened by chance, have lacked the wisdom, the thinking, and the tenacity that such initiatives demand. The Church needs a *policy* of engagement, and to make provision for skilled personnel to serve it.

The possibilities through such initiatives are immense, and the immediate objectives are clear – to make easy and informal contact with the institutions of society, to listen and to learn, to sow ideas, to get people together to think and talk about their own professional concerns and the wider context in which they are set – with relevant Christian insights disclosed in the course of that dialogue, as happens inevitably as men pursue at depth their own secular concern. One thinks o f many examples, of the way that Industrial Mission has led to many ongoing groups of men meeting; directors meeting to discuss aspects of industrial organization that would rarely find place in the board room, young managers facing controversial issues that the pressures of administration would never allow at the works, shop stewards and union men looking at aspects of industrial problems not easily studied in the branch meetings, and so on. Inevitably, on the job, the more leisurely study of issues, their background and wider context, the philosophy of things, can hardly find place. But such opportunities are far from matters of leisure – and men can see it.

But industry, though basic is only one institution of modern society. In some urban centres, it is now customary for the Church – through competent agents – to bring together men and women, such as children's officers, probation officers, almoners, and all kinds of social workers to confer about social problems and human beings. It is utterly impossible for such dialogue to take place without the Christian understanding of man and society being raised. Again there are 'frontier' meetings with city councillors and local government officers, with teachers, dialogue between clergy, doctors and psychiatrists as is visualized by the new Institute of Religion and Medicine, and so on. . . . It is not easy to bring such groups into being, but sufficient of them now exist to show the tremendous possibilities if the Church more generally were to see this dimension of mission and ministry.

This is the modern mode of engagement of the Church with the 'principalities and powers' of modern society; that is to say, we are not thinking of bishops on the Coal Board! That engagement, whether with industry, Trades Unions, local councillors, professional social workers, a government department, a College of Advanced Technology, whatever the institution, requires skilful instruments, highly-trained men and women, lay and ordained, with some specialized competence, who can establish informal and easy relationships and stimulate this 'frontier' dialogue. It *is* the

task of a Church, in an age weighed down with the demands
for minute machine-drawings in our technological, planned
and partly-planned society to raise the issues of the larger
canvas, of the kind of society we should seek, in the light of the
deepest requirements of human and social well-being. Such
encounter therefore should be closely concerned with social
goals, the human and social consequences of technical decisions,
a right orientation of society and its institutions, subjecting
them to the critique of the best thinking. Properly, such
initiatives and dialogue should be ecumenical in spirit, induc-
tive in relation to Christian faith – rather than deductive –
secular in their concern. To the extent that ordained men are
engaged in these initiatives – and they have an important part
to play – they are essentially ancillary: the operation is essentially the concern of the laity, of ordinary people, at all levels,
being deeply and responsibly involved in their own affairs.
The Church, not just because she is the Church or because she
'knows the answers', but because she is supposed to be wise
about a certain way of life, has a real role in the creation of a
good and responsible society. For a National Church it is a
moral obligation to fulfil that role. But she cannot do it without a determined policy.

Can it Happen?

Can the Church of England secure this 'new look'? Can
she adopt the kind of policy and strategy that would give
meaningful content to a genuine Establishment of the Christian
religion, even in a missionary situation? It would be a massive
undertaking for so large, undefined and unorganized a body
as the Church of England. Nor could it happen all at once,
even if the will and determination existed. Clear leadership
would be imperative, and we may believe that the response to
it would be considerable, from clergy and lay-people, from
within the Church and from many outside. We may believe
too, that if there is little articulated *will* that the Church should
engage the national life the *wish* that she should do so is

more common than we think, and again, both within the Church and outside. But wishing is notoriously inadequate. The problem then would be to know what steps might be needed to shift the Church in this direction, whether there are things, practical things that we can do to strengthen or even to begin that sustained process of engagements. I submit that there are certainly three modest requirements that would be essential preliminaries, and I conclude this essay with setting them out.

First, may it humbly be suggested that the leadership of the Church, which includes more than the bishops, but notably includes the bishops, must have a clear recognition, in broad outline, of both the need, and the details of a policy and strategy of engagement? The 'judicious' Hooker writing on a national church felt obliged to make a 'respectful admonition to the prelates of England'. Today again, the question of the role of episcopacy in the contemporary Church has been raised, and it is a crucial one for the issues we are concerned with in this thesis. A study of the historic role of bishops shows that their pre-eminence as chief pastors and fathers-in-God, as presidents at the Liturgy and symbols of unity did not exhaust their functions. In Christendom these became the normative ones but if we go far back there was another. Pre-eminently the bishop was a missionary, pressing on into new territory, encountering new principalities and powers, and leaving behind him (unless he were martyred!) 'churches' and 'parishes'. Before there were dioceses in England, there were missions headed by bishops. This is only another way of saying they were strategists of mission in the society of their time, concerned with cultural penetration no less than with territorial expansion. In any institution requiring fresh orientation, the leadership is of crucial importance. If we admit that the contemporary Church faces an acute mission situation, and that a National Church certainly has a paramount responsibility to engage the national life, it is vitally important that the apostolic function be construed in terms of missionary strategy.

Secondly, in any planned strategy, bishops and the Church at large need expert assistance. The mission of a genuinely National Church needs something like a 'research and development' group at its centre to undertake the necessary sociological and basic study of the operation of engagement and mission. The matters are legion on which intelligent planning must be informed. Just to illustrate with a few examples: What are the steps whereby an activated laity can be called out, trained and sustained in the task of mission and engagement? How can the Church be helped to the necessary orientation of mind and the appropriate spirituality for this task? What structure of pastoral care must we devise to hold and bring through to mature conviction the newly-confirmed, so to staunch the largest flow of life-blood from the body of the Church; not solely for the Church, but that they may be able to live wholly committed to the world, yet as Christian men and women? At what strategic points should we seek engagement with the institutions of society, and how is it done? What re-shaping of territorial boundaries, of parishes, deaneries, and very important in the light of the local government re-organization and regional developments, of dioceses do we need to secure effective missionary units, *zones humaines* as the French Catholic sociologists call them? And so on. . . . These are not questions to be answered by the light of nature, or by revelation: they require study, careful experimentation, the collation of experience. The hard strategy of engagement as we have delineated it would entail facing them. Such a 'research and development' group might replace some of the overlapping and unwieldy committee structure of the Church Assembly. It could be set up quickly and at little cost.

Thirdly, at the service of a policy of engagement, in all its range, there is the need for some highly-skilled practitioners. They are in short supply even to meet existent needs of the Church. Already we know that it is intensely difficult to find men for Industrial Mission work, to find men who can win a relevant ministry, in, say, the world of technical and further education, to work with Frontier groups, to serve the Christian interests in television companies, and so on. The few that are proven are simply inundated with offers of jobs and demands for their services. We simply do not train men for these jobs. And for the traditional ministry all our training is of a similar kind – pre-medical and for general practice, rather than post-graduate and specialist. The missionary parish, certainly the heading-up of 'major parishes' requires far more than our normal theological education provides. It is really quite extraordinary that in a period when every kind of intellectual discipline is breaking the knowledge barrier, discovering new specialisms, and proliferating institutes for advanced education, theological education and practical training for the ministry of the Church should all be at the same general – and not very high – level, with the same, monochrome – and not very imaginative – content. We shall not augment the number of skilled practitioners in engagement without, certainly, one of our colleges being set aside to train them – ordained men, lay-men and women. It would be a kind of Staff Training College, essentially 'post-graduate', specialized, marked by an appropriate theological edge and orientation for mission in a secular society. It would not simply be an academic institution, but closely geared into the strategical planning of the Church in relation to different areas of the national life.

These three steps – a determined mind and will in the leadership of the Church, a research and development group, a Staff Training College – may sound prosaic and unduly ecclesiastical when one thinks of the enormous task in hand, the large canvas of engagement we have painted. That is so. But they are basic steps to be taken and they are concrete things that could happen, more important than many high-sounding resolutions. The Church's integrity is to be tested by doing concrete, if seemingly modest things. But of course, they are means, not ends. The end is a lively enlightened Christian conscience in the nation, a ferment of new thinking and bold initiative, a renewed Church at the service of Christ and His world. Bishop Westcott once wrote 'It is the office of the State to give effect to public opinion: it is the office of the Church to shape it.' When we grasp that the Church is the laity dispersed into all the different areas of secular life, we may see the high ends which the prosaic administrative decisions in the Church have to serve.

This essay has dealt with the strategy and structure of the Church if she is to engage the national life in a serious way. I have submitted that to do this is a *sine qua non* of a National Church, and gives meaning, content and substance to the Establishment of the Christian religion. It aims precisely at Establishment in the most genuine meaning of that word, and if the formula of Establishment does not symbolize this, then it is empty, if not profane. Perhaps, in the judgement and providence of God, it is already too late for this to happen, in which case the sooner it becomes clear, the better surely, in order that the Church may be rid of illusion, cleansed, and in the mercy of God, respond to a new situation. But we do not know this yet. Our task surely even at this late hour is to act in obedience to such understanding as we can have of the calling of a National Church.

There are of course other questions of immense importance that we have not touched upon that bear on these issues, though some are implicit in this essay. What is the Word of God for our time and place? An important question indeed for a National Church, and not simply answered from our abiding knowledge of the revealed truths of the Christian religion. What are the things that belong to our peace as a national community in the world of the sixties? How do we express and communicate Christian truth to men for whom the 'vertical' dimension is blurred – as it must be, by definition, for the run of men in a secular society? To these hard questions the Church also needs provisional answers – discoverable, probably, only in the struggle for engagement and dialogue with the secular society in which she lives. But we have all the time been speaking of the Reformation of the Church, and all reformation means struggle, and all reformation requires spiritual, theological and intellectual renaissance.

NOTES

1. Lewis Mumford, *The Culture of Cities*, p. 74.
2. Richard Hooker, *The Laws of Ecclesiastical Polity*, Book 8.
3. Teilhard de Chardin, *Le Milieu Divin*, pp. 38–9.

For the argument in this chapter see Bishop Wickham's second book, *Encounter with Modern Society*.

CONCLUSIONS

IN this short book the writers have tried to appraise, from their several points of view, the situation and responsibility of the Church of England in the nation's life at the present time. They believe that in consequence of the church–state relationship which is its inheritance the Church of England is better poised than any other body or group to grapple with that situation and exercise that responsibility. It cannot of course go it alone. Just as in a big city, town council, university and schools, industry and commerce, and Church, represent the major influences and should be four partners converging upon the life of the city, similarly in a country and the world. And if the Church is to do its part it must be the whole Church in unison; and therefore its members can no longer tolerate complacently its divisions.

All this requires of the Church of England in particular, a more thorough-going change in thought, temper, and practice than it has been able hitherto to achieve; and unless this change happens quickly it may be too late. The national Church has to realize in all its parts and pieces and to the very heart of its being that it is confronted with a new situation here and now in England as is the Church in other countries.

The situation is in many respects as much a missionary one as when Aidan set foot in Northumbria in A.D. 635 and William the Conqueror set foot in Sussex in 1066 and sent as soon as he could for Lanfranc to come and reform the Anglo-Saxon Church. Now, as then, internal reform, missionary penetration and pastoral ministry march together. Missionary work and a pastoral ministry as the Gospels show are not alternatives. Indeed a care for all men, as unbounded as the love of Christ Jesus, has always been a more persuasive demonstration of that love than any amount of talking. The greatest failure of the national church in the eighteenth century and since at the parish level was because its pastoral ministry was too often cold in temper; limited to a select few and careless of the many, while bishops and deans who, may indeed have entered into dialogue with the men of power, also were aloof from the people and shut away trying to keep themselves warm in their draughty palaces and deaneries. The manual workers have long memories. We have much to live down.

The Church has to become through and through a society that has a care and concern for the people of England. Its top priority is not a campaign for membership and subscriptions, but a strategy of penetration motivated by the Gospel of the Kingdom of God and faith in Jesus Christ. The Christian enterprise required today, however, is more difficult and complex than it was in early days. The Church is no longer a visible unity in England and the world, which its Lord said it must be in order to convince the world that he is Saviour and Lord. Social life is more complicated; the population has enormously increased and is much more mobile. The average length of life has more than doubled and people are less concerned than in former days with what will happen to them after death – in spite of the prodigious slaughter of young men in two successive world wars. As a result of the scientific revolution, society has very nearly passed from the agricultural age, which still influences thought-forms and poetic imagery, into an industrial and technological era, in which thought-forms and poetic imagery will in time be different. There are other ideologies, scientific, humanist, atheist, which are penetrating deep into society and the Church itself.

In a thousand years church and society have collected a lot of impedimenta. The left luggage of establishment has overspilled on to the platforms and even the track. Much of it is not only in the way but must be got out of the way. Many members of the ecclesiastical trade union, which is one of the oldest, are content to look busy and feel busy, pushing the impedimenta about on the platform or lifting a piece which has fallen on the track back on to the platform. A mentality adapted to a static and agricultural age is not adapted to a mobile and industrial age. Before the Church tries to argue with contemporary society, therefore, it must listen to what the Spirit is saying through science and technology, art and literature, and in the movement from individualism to community. The Christian ministry has to face the fact of the break away from traditions, habits and style of life which have up till now been accepted, and which have, rightly or wrongly, been assumed to be Christian. Whether we like it or not, modern man is becoming estranged from many inherited customs and pre-suppositions. Therefore the Church, in order to be an effective influence in the new era, will have to make a true appraisal of the constituents of secularization and also have the courage to reformulate some of its traditional beliefs and to re-affirm others – always mindful of the wise distinction made by the philosopher, A. N. Whitehead, that 'the dogmatic finality of *verbal* expression is a mistaken notion'.

Given a revival of conviction and a care for humanity, has the membership of the Church also the resolve to re-deploy its existing resources realistically? This would mean making its financial resources flexible and more mobile. The minor but overdue constitutional reforms proposed by the Crown Appointments Commission should become operative without undue delay, and likewise the reshaping of the pattern of the Church's organization – without swamping the merits of episcopacy and of diocesan freedom by bureaucracy and over-centralization. The laity of the Church also must be intelligent about their faith, and become a spear-head of the Church's penetration of society as well as sharing responsibility in the constitutional life of the Church. But let us not imagine this or some form of presbyterianism is the remedy for anglican ills. Nonconformity where the laity are more in control has had a disastrous slump and the presbyterian Church in Scotland as elsewhere has not escaped a sleepy sickness.

While it is impossible to say that there is only one remedy for the weakness of an organism which has many parts and operations or that there is only one way of making a massive penetration of society, be it in England or central Africa, nevertheless a *sine qua non* in the life and work of a Church is the quality of its ordained ministry and its numerical sufficiency for the work it has to do at home and overseas. In the calling and training of men and women the Church of England, for one, has not been imaginative, radical and far-seeing. There has been, and is, a lot of talk, a lot of waste, a terrible record of hesitation and failure.

So what? The Church will have to do everything it can to draw into its ministry a larger number of men, and I would also say of women, of mental ability and conviction. The more alert it is in its encounter with modern society, as Bishop Wickham is saying, the more likely is this to happen. The work of the ministry has rarely, if ever, been so difficult – or so rewarding as it is today. Men of promise should be encouraged, and given incentives to read for an honours degree in one of the major subjects – both science and arts – and to go flat out to get the highest class of which they are capable. That achieved, they should spend another two years at a university – here or in another country – in taking an honours degree in theology with clear reference to contemporary thought and society. It is essential that they should study theology in a university where they can rub their minds against those of students in other faculties.

There are also many men of intelligence who will not make much showing at academic studies and many of these may care greatly for their fellow-men and love God. With an appropriate training and the discipline of hard work they will become excellent priests, pastors and missionaries in a secular society. But often in England for one reason or other men who could and should be intelligent about their jobs and thoughtful, are mishandled in their training and allowed to become stupid, and so they become lazy and slothful as the years pass. We do not yet seem to have got the educational expertise for bringing the best out of such men and women.

Then, the university stage or its equivalent completed, a

definitely clinical training such as doctors have will follow: to learn the disciplined life and practice which a priest must have to see him through his ministry, to study the techniques of group discussion, teaching and preaching, the expertise of varied pastoral work, the rudiments of administration and of being handy about the house and not wasting time and money; to be reminded that he will be ordained to a ministry in the Church of God and therefore should, like men in the fighting services, be ready to serve in any part of the world. Normally but by no means invariably for all ordinands, the most convenient way of doing this is in a 'theological college'. For this period of clinical training, which could be less dilatory than it is at present, there are four essentials: those who direct and give it should be experts, not educational amateurs; the corporate life should be shared with Christians who are going to lay jobs in the world – this might reduce clerical gossip in common rooms to a minimum; many months before this intensive training, and in the vacations during it, should be devoted to gaining experience of the world in which the parson will have to operate, e.g. as a wage-earner on the shop-floor of industry, the docks, or in a ship, or in the social services, or in another country learning thoroughly a foreign language. And fourthly in some centres men should be trained for special ministries at home and overseas instead of training everyone as a general practitioner: industrial missionaries, university, hospital and school chaplains, service and prison chaplains, teaching and youth work, and, at a later stage, spiritual direction and marriage guidance. And in all this, learning not to waste time, and yet to appear to have time to listen to the people he encounters. The clergy unfortunately have a reputation for being lazy which some of their number have earned for them. The only way to get rid of it is to be both hard-working and keen on the job and to care for people. But many, alas, lose this keenness early because they have no idea how to tackle it – their 'training' having been too imprecise to help them.

Here, too, the laity could help. A man engaged in an exacting job needs, after a period of years, a long sabbatical term – for taking stock, for uninterrupted study, for improving his expertise, to get away quietly from the world of men to the world of nature, and from the daily chores to the rest of God in order to return to serve better and more confidently. The Church should provide this and pay the cost. At present it doesn't. One can get money for buildings, and for the perpetuation of a lot of obsolete organization, but it is hard to get sufficient money to help the ministry to be at its best and to give of its best. Why this dullness among church members in regard to priorities of giving? Probably because there is nothing to show for it whereas one can point to a stained-glass window, an organ or new buildings.

Finally, one would propose that every man when he is accepted conditionally for ordination should be attached from then onwards to a bishop – partly of his choosing – without being committed to the diocese where the bishop happens to be serving. If every ordinand had to keep in touch with a particular bishop, two or three times a year right through his training, and if every bishop operating in the country (there are more than 130 in England alone) had a dozen or so ordinands who made contact with him as they moved towards ordination, it would be good for the bishops and good for the ordinands and would strengthen and deepen the kind of personal relationship which should exist in an episcopal church.

These concrete proposals in regard to the ministry, are integral to a discussion of 'The New Look' – because the mentality and temper of any society, especially a church, are most strongly influenced by its whole-time officers who so to say have the keys. The ecclesiastical laity may talk their heads off about the ministry of the laity, lay training and all – fair enough, but indisputably not enough unless the full-time and ordained ministry is first-rate and therefore welcomes the co-operation of other laymen and women and is not so depleted in numbers that it is spread too thinly over the fields of opportunity. And even that is not all.

'The spirit of man is the candle of the Lord', said a wise man long ago. The spirit of man is being hard put to digest all the new matter that science, psychology and technology are feeding into him. The process of gestation and assimilation will take a long time. No one can foresee what changes secularization, automation, and nuclear energy will bring about. Some of the dehumanizing features of industry and economic competition may disappear but other evils may take their place and the drift towards atheism might become a landslide if the Church became only a marginal influence. Unless the new-won leisure and affluence are civilized and men learn to live in obedience to the Divine Imperative the result might be an irretrievable catastrophe to the human race. That being man's predicament the Church would fail humanity if church men and women were so busy in good works and salesmanship and in encounters with secular society that their spirituality was not being renewed and deepened by encounter with the living God.

When a man is honest with himself, and sees himself in a mirror for what he is (or a community with itself) it is a little fellow that he sees for all his panache and self-sufficiency, short-lived and self-centred – what I would not that I do, and all that – and at his shoulder evil, a hideous, inexplicable power in life. In that moment of realism he wants to be assured that truth and love endure, that the Christ who died on the Cross is alive and that the Kingdom where the supremacy of truth and love are undisputed by pride or any evil is the end towards which the cosmos moves. It is this faith and hope in the gracious purpose of God that a national Church, its spirituality deep-set and its heart warmed by the all-embracing love of Christ, has to be infusing into the life of a nation and nations – not man-made, but God-given. Its source of renewal not just a linking up with the *activity* of God in the world, as it were the 'daemon' of secularization, but the reality of the abiding God. 'The existence of a personal Reality sufficiently like us to be able to penetrate and move us through and through . . . is the original and persistent cause of this noblest dissatisfaction with anything and all things merely human.'. . .

CONCLUSIONS

'We are not God, Yet how we need Him! And this, then, not as just a larger ourselves, not as a larger Becoming, but as Being, as Joy, Pure and Undefiled.' So wrote a great, far-sighted Christian forty-five years ago.*

From that time on many of his disciples withdrew and no longer went about with him. So Jesus asked the Twelve, do you also want to leave me? Simon Peter answered, Lord to whom shall we go? Your words are words of eternal life.

* The two quotations are from Baron Frederick von Hügel and are included in *Spiritual Counsels and Letters*, selected with an introduction by Douglas V. Steere. Darton, Longman & Todd, 1964. The passage from Scripture is St John, 6, 66–8. N.E.B. translation.

APPENDIX: THE WRITERS

EDWARD FREDERICK CARPENTER
M.A., B.D. Lond. Fellow of King's College. Vicar of Stanmore 1945–51; Canon of Westminster 1951–63. Archdeacon since 1963. Chairman London Society for the Study of Religion. Author of several books, of which one published this year is *The Service of a Parson*.

LESLIE STANNARD HUNTER
M.A. Oxon. Hon. D.C.L. Durham. D.D. Toronto. LL.D. Sheffield. Vicar of Barking 1926–30. Archdeacon of Northumberland 1931–9. Chaplain to the King 1936. Bishop of Sheffield 1939–62. Chairman of William Temple College and of C. of E. Industrial Committee. Author and editor of several books, two published this year being *A Diocesan Service Book* and *The Scandinavian Churches*.

ALFRED JOWETT
M.A. Hons. and Cert. in Education, Camb. Vicar of St George's, Sheffield 1951–60. Vicar of Doncaster and Hon. Canon of Sheffield 1960–64. Dean of Manchester since 1964.

THEODORE RICHARD MILFORD
M.A. Oxon. Lecturer St John's College, Agra 1931–5. A Secretary of the Student Christian Movement 1924–6, 1935–8. Vicar of St Mary's (Univ. Ch.) Oxon 1938–47. Canon and Chancellor of Lincoln 1947–8. Since then Master of the Temple. Chairman of Oxfam.

MAX ALEXANDER CUNNINGHAM WARREN
M.A. Camb. Hon. D.D. Toronto. Vicar of Holy Trinity, Camb. 1936–42. General Secretary of the Church Mission Society 1942–62. Now Canon of Westminster. Author of several books, of which the latest is *The Functions of a National Church*, Epworth Press 1964, 5/-.

EDWARD RALPH WICKHAM
B.D. London. Diocesan Missioner to Industry, Diocese of Sheffield, 1944–59. Canon of Sheffield 1951–9. Suffragan Bishop of Middleton from 1959. Author of *Church and People in an Industrial City* and *Encounter with Modern Society*, Lutterworth Press.